Collaboration and Innov
in Criminal Justice

Drawing on original research on community-based alternatives to offender rehabilitation, this book provides an up-to-date depiction of the challenges faced by front-line workers at the interface between criminal justice and welfare systems striving to address needs and provide multifaceted solutions.

Using an innovative theoretical approach predicated on activity theory (AT) to dissect the problem, the book makes the case for co-created rehabilitation strategies that address the needs of offenders – which can only be achieved with the involvement of health and social welfare services as a means to provide a holistic support to individuals – and regard for the dilemmas front-line professionals face to deploy such strategies – which means shifting the top-down paradigm of policy implementation for co-created solutions. The book explores how AT can be used to help design commensurate interventions that give voice to all the interested actors involved in the rehabilitation process and provide readers with tools that help translate theory into practice.

This book is essential reading for students, researchers, practitioners and other stakeholders focusing on co-created, bottom-up alternatives to imprisonment that benefit both offenders, community and the state.

Paulo Rocha is an attorney specialising in international law with a PhD in social sciences obtained at the University of Stavanger, Norway. His research interests are collaboration and innovation strategies in the public sector. He is the author of "Performance-Based Policy in Offender Rehabilitation" and "Tracing the Historical Development of a Service Model for Interagency Collaboration," among other papers.

Routledge Frontiers of Criminal Justice

For more information about this series, please visit: www.routledge.com/ Routledge-Frontiers-of-Criminal-Justice/book-series/RFCJ

Collaboration and Innovation in Criminal Justice

An Activity Theory Alternative to Offender Rehabilitation

Paulo Rocha

Routledge
Taylor & Francis Group
LONDON AND NEW YORK

First published 2022
by Routledge
2 Park Square, Milton Park, Abingdon, Oxon OX14 4RN

and by Routledge
605 Third Avenue, New York, NY 10158

Routledge is an imprint of the Taylor & Francis Group, an informa business

British Library Cataloguing-in-Publication Data
A catalogue record for this book is available from the British Library

Library of Congress Cataloging-in-Publication Data
A catalog record for this book has been requested

ISBN: 978-1-032-03336-5 (hbk)
ISBN: 978-1-032-03337-2 (pbk)
ISBN: 978-1-003-18679-3 (ebk)

DOI: 10.4324/9781003186793

Typeset in Times New Roman
by Apex CoVantage, LLC

Contents

Figures and tables

Figures

Tables

Abbreviations

AT   Activity theory
CHAT   Cultural-historical activity theory
CLM   Change laboratory model
GP   General practitioner
IT   Information technology
L&D   Liaison and diversion services
NHS   National Health Service
NPM   New Public Management
UK   United Kingdom
USA   United States of America

Acknowledgements

Several years back, I learned to be wary of acknowledging any, let alone all, of those who had any contribution to my work. Not because I am ungrateful to them but because I am reticent to compile a list of people who might subsequently be accused of being guilty parties. Although I have been extremely grateful for a vast number of conversations I have had with people across multiple contexts during the research and writing of this book, I would like – above all – to thank sincerely my friends and family, especially my wife Kasia, my children Filip and Klara and my parents Maria and Hindemburgo. You have supported me throughout this journey, and because of you, everything has had a meaning.

Yet there are more people I will name because a number of ideas present in this book have been best honed by their testing on their brilliant minds. Of all the people from whom I have benefited when discussing the topics of this book, no one has opened my mind more often than Dr. Sarah Hean, Dr. Ann-Karin Holmen, Dr. Reidar Staupe and Stan Sadler. I am happy to credit any of my better observations to them while insisting that any of the worst are mine.

This book was an outcome of a project that received funding from the European Union's Horizon 2020 research and innovation programme under the Marie Skłodowska-Curie grant agreement No. 734536. A special thanks to all the staff of the liaison and diversion agency that was part of this study.

Paulo Rocha,
April, 2021

1 Introduction

Understanding offender rehabilitation

1.1 Empirical background

Offender rehabilitation is a strategy of paramount importance that the criminal justice system uses to promote the reintegration of individuals into the community (Armstrong & McNeill, 2012; Ministry of Justice UK, 2013). In this vein, motivating offenders to engage in rehabilitative interventions is a key step toward their potential desistance from further criminal behaviour (Fazel & Danesh, 2002; Fazel & Wolf, 2015; World Health Organization, 2005). As inmates are three times more likely to struggle with multiple vulnerabilities (which includes, for example, mental health problems, substance misuse and learning disabilities) than the population in general (Sinha, 2010), commensurate rehabilitation strategies ought to tackle clusters of correlated needs and provide multifaceted solutions (Andrews & Bonta, 2016). To that end, the involvement of professionals from multiple areas of care in the rehabilitation process is pivotal to enhance people's odds of remaining crime free (Hean et al., 2009; Strype et al., 2014).

Policymakers worldwide strive to produce adequate policies that progress integrated care organised between criminal justice and welfare services (Department i Helse og Omsorg, 2013; Department of Health, 2010; World Health Organization, 2015). When interagency collaboration engenders co-provided care, mental health outcomes improve, reoffending rates decrease and the financial costs incurred by the taxpayers supporting prison and health services drop (Bond & Gittell, 2010). The challenge, however, is that policymakers and service leaders have focused on generic integration strategies that overlook the reality existent at street level, such as the misalignment of organisational working schedules, logistical issues and limited resources (Rocha & Holmen, 2020).

This book reflects on a case study was conducted in the context of offender rehabilitation in England and Wales to explore the perspective of frontline workers across criminal justice and welfare systems. The focus of the study was on a public service called Criminal Justice Liaison and Diversion

DOI: 10.4324/9781003186793-1

(L&D), an organisation that supports vulnerable offenders when they are first in touch with the criminal justice system (e.g., police custody and court) by diverting them, if appropriate, to health and other care services as early as possible in their trajectory through criminal justice (James, 1999). As such, L&D is a model of funding, administration, organisation, service delivery and care designed to engender connectivity, alignment and collaboration within and between differentiated sectors (Kodner & Spreeuwenberg, 2002).

For over three decades, L&D services have been locally managed (Reed, 1992), which has produced varied results across sites. During this time, however, the national government has recurrently attempted to unify L&D practice over England (James, 1999). In its most recent attempt, the government has commissioned a review to assess the condition of people with mental health problems or learning disabilities in the criminal justice system (Carter, 2007), which resulted in a report (Bradley, 2009) confirming the relevance of L&D services at both police custody and courts to divert vulnerable individuals into care (McGilloway & Donnelly, 2004). Based on the findings of the review, policymakers and service leaders developed a national model for L&D services intending to unify practice across the sites (NHS England Liaison and Diversion Programme, 2014). The document specifies outcomes to be equally achieved nationwide and bases the funding of local services according to their performance. This formula was initially implemented in a few forerunner locations (called "wave one" sites) in England on April 2014 and has, ever since, been spread across all the sites.

In light of this, this book investigates how interagency collaboration between L&D and neighbouring services has been perceived by street-level L&D workers after the introduction of the new national model for liaison and diversion services. The focus is pointedly on the perspective of front-line workers to explore a different angle regarding models of interagency collaboration across criminal justice and welfare systems, as traditional research is prone to focus on service-level outcomes (Parker et al., 2018). In other words, by investigating the perspective of L&D front-line workers on the role of the service as a bridge between criminal justice and welfare services, this book is an attempt to develop a better understanding as to why interagency collaboration is still challenging to achieve at the street level despite the willingness demonstrated by organisations to work in tandem.

1.2 Theoretical background: interagency collaboration in offender rehabilitation

Interagency collaboration has been widely suggested as an appropriate means to address the challenges of vulnerable individuals coming in contact with the criminal justice system by the scientific literature (Department i

Helse og Omsorg, 2013; Department of Health, 2010; World Health Organization, 2015). Notwithstanding, readers striving to make sense of the topic might find themselves dumbfounded by the wide range of interchangeable terms loosely adopted to explain the same phenomenon, that is, organisations working in tandem. This creates a conundrum for those attempting to differentiate interorganisational relationships from interagency collaboration. Terms such as interagency, multiagency and multisectoral, for instance, have been used to describe the relationship between different organisations (Statham, 2011; Williams, 2012). Moreover, terms such as cooperation, collaboration, coordination and integration have been adopted to describe the increasing levels of formalisation that such relationship embodies. Table 1.1 exemplifies the multiple levels of interagency working.

This streamlined taxonomy serves to illustrate why it is possible to observe in the literature a degree of interchangeability among the mentioned terms, that is, the transferable characteristics to be equally observed in every joint initiative: information sharing, common decision-making and coordinated interventions (Statham, 2011).

In England and Wales, public policy has followed these notions and promoted various collaboration models to be operationalised by agencies in both criminal justice and welfare systems (UK Crown, 2007; Department of Health, 2013; Department of Health and Concordat Signatories, 2014; Home Office UK, 2014; Home Office, 2015; Home Office Department of Health, 2000). The shared goal of these models has been to improve health and social care outcomes for individuals and lowering service costs, which should be facilitated by information sharing, common decision-making and coordinated interventions (Home Office UK, 2014).

In other areas, the idea is the same. Models of collaboration between criminal justice and welfare systems, which generally tend to focus on prearrest/pre-sentence interventions to avoid unnecessary incarcerations (Earl et al., 2015; Herrington et al., 2009; Winters et al., 2015), also prioritise information sharing and integrated care, usually organised between

Table 1.1 Increasing levels of formalisation (Frost, 2005)

Label	Features
Cooperation	Organisations working together, but independently, to achieve consistent goals and provide complementary services
Collaboration	Organisations working jointly to address the shared goal of mitigating issues of duplication and/or gaps in service provision
Coordination	Organisations working together in a planned and systematic fashion to achieve agreed-upon and shared objectives
Integration	Different organisations merging to enhance service delivery

the police and services in both criminal justice and welfare systems. In the literature, there is a lot written, for example, about the crisis intervention team, an American-based model of collaboration that qualifies police officers to manage vulnerable individuals and to provide them with treatment instead of arrest (Boscarato et al., 2014; (Laign et al., 2009; Winters et al., 2015). However, other models of prearrest/pre-sentence collaboration can also be found in Australia (Herrington et al., 2009), Canada (Winters et al., 2015) and the USA (Clayfield et al., 2005).

In England and Wales, there are studies done on both information sharing within welfare services and between welfare agencies and organisations in other sectors (Jenkins, 2014). Besides, there is also research on interagency work in the context of offender rehabilitation (Atkinson et al., 2007; Oliver et al., 2010; Phillips et al., 2000; Williams, 2009) and even on models of collaboration involving the police and mental health care organisations (Parker et al., 2018). Among the reported (James et al., 2010; Earl et al., 2015; Great Britain Home Office, 2015), the Criminal Justice Liaison and Diversion was a prominent example of collaboration attempting to avoid unnecessary imprisonment. In contrast with the crisis intervention team in the USA, L&D relies on the introduction of specialists in police custody and court settings to provide on-site assistance to criminal justice professionals in their goal to identify and support vulnerable individuals (NHS England Liaison and Diversion Programme, 2014).

Another particularity observed upon a review of the literature was the proclivity to suggest interagency collaboration as a means to tackle the inaptitude of criminal justice front-line workers to independently address the needs of vulnerable people (Fenge et al., 2014). In this aspect, researchers emphasise that it would be expected from professionals in the police and court to be trained to recognise and handle vulnerable individuals, since they are often the first public services to interact with people, but studies have shown that vulnerabilities are often unrecognised or poorly handled by front-line professionals in criminal justice systems. The consequence is the imprisonment of people who should be otherwise treated in the community. Hence the understanding that the involvement of welfare workers is crucial to improve health and social care outcomes (Sainsbury Centre for Mental Health, 2009).

Above all, however, it is possible to notice that most of the studies are constrained to a perfunctory analysis limited to reporting and/or describing the existent collaboration models. There seems to be no scope for a deeper analysis of these collaboration models, despite their current implementation within policing. Furthermore, a considerable part of the literature seems to prioritise organisational/service-level outcomes (e.g., arrest rates, diversion rates and referrals to other services) as the parameters for assessment of the eventual success of the models and end up belittling the relevance of the role played by workers at the street level (Parker et al., 2018). In this sense, this book focuses on the perspective of front-line workers in response to the mentioned gap in the literature and offers more than a simple description of collaboration models. It explores the challenges of interagency collaboration realised at the street level, and it does so by innovatively using activity theory to make sense of the state of affairs.

1.2.1 The role of front-line workers in interagency collaboration and policy implementation

The idea that criminal justice services ought to collaborate with other agencies in the welfare sector in response to the increasing number of vulnerable individuals in the prison population is widely championed across countries. However, the operationalisation of such an objective does not seem to be straightforward. Traditionally, top-down policies are enacted by central levels of government to foster collaboration between organisations across sectors. Governments tend to surmise that these injunctions will be naturally picked up by workers at the street level of public service organisations and make no contingency plans. The challenge, however, is that generally circumstances occurring at the street level hamper the uncomplicated dissemination of policy instructions (Hill & Huppe, 2014).

In this book, the concepts "front-line workers" or "street-level professionals, staff and employees" are adopted interchangeably and refer to street-level bureaucrats in the public service sectors (Lipsky, 2010). According to Lipsky, street-level bureaucrats are employees at the operational level of public service organisations who are in direct contact with the public and benefit from a certain degree of discretion in their decision-making processes regarding issues of service provision (Lipsky, 2010). These professionals are continuously developing coping mechanisms to square top-down expectations and limited resources in the daily work, which turns them into factual policymakers with a strong capacity to sway policy implementation (Lipsky, 2010).

The introduction of new solutions in the public sector through top-down policy is harshly contested in the literature (see, e.g., Fuglsang, 2010; Lippke & Wegener, 2014). This is especially true in cases where policies introduce a performance-based approach to stimulate implementation. Performance-based policy can be understood as the use of remuneration to motivate public organisations to achieve desired goals (Herbst, 2007), something that is rather controversial among scholars. Fuglsang (2010), for instance, defends that new ideas in the public sector should emerge through interaction and not being imposed top-down with the use of remuneration as a stimulator. Similarly, Clarke (2013, p. 111) states that the economic strains imposed by performance-based policies tend to force front-line workers to be rebellious if they want to "establish a culture where creative thinking and reflective practice can inform delivering a service that better understands the individual and supports their efforts to rebuild their lives." It is in this scenario that the notion of street-level bureaucracy becomes crucial. In fact, Lipsky's theory is most likely to have endured over the years exactly because he was able to capture and articulate the bureaucratic hurdles encountered by front-line workers who strive to equate top-down policies with their responsibilities at the street level.

Although the idea of coping mechanisms (i.e., responses developed by street-level bureaucrats to deal with the obstacles caused by sparse resources, few controls, indeterminate objectives and discouraging circumstances) is still adequate in today's public administration and instantiates the role of street-level bureaucrats, it is also judicious to adapt this notion to current practice by expanding on the street-level bureaucracy literature. Traditionally, there was an empirical focus on front-line workers operating within the boundaries of their own professional fields, for example, social workers allocating care payments (Ellis, 2007), cops policing the streets, teachers teaching school children and counsellors providing vocational rehabilitation support (Maynard-Moody & Musheno, 2003). However, the current scenario is that street-level operations are most likely to transcend the boundaries of a specific professional field and require workers to collaborate with each other beyond the limits of their own organisations as part of the street-level bureaucratic process. Indeed, the whole notion of integrated care collaboratively provided by agencies across criminal justice and welfare systems is predicated on such a setup, which confirms the need to break away from the legacy approach to street-level bureaucracy within organisational boundaries. Because the traditional perspective of street-level bureaucracy seems to constrain its analysis to practices within the limits of a specific professional field (Hupe, 2014; Hupe & Hill, 2016), the overlap between interagency collaboration and street-level bureaucracy is still underexplored. Thus, this book contributes to filling a theoretical gap in both the interagency collaboration and the street-level bureaucracy literature by investigating the role of street-level bureaucrats in the realisation of collaboration between agencies.

1.2.2 Interagency collaboration through co-creation in the public sector

The public sector has been undergoing structural transformations in recent years, transitioning from a legal authority into an environment for co-creation. Such a shift can be construed as an attempt to fill the void left since the demise of the new public management (NPM; Hood & Dixon, 2015). The approach, which has been deemed inadequate in light of today's demands, can still be observed in practice, though.

Traditionally, NPM is predicated on the adoption of lean technologies to boost cost-efficiency and cure the perils linked with the classical public bureaucracy. The caveat is its limited long-term impact, since additional gains in efficiency and effectiveness tend to become sparse after the initial effect of the strategy is over (Radnor & Osborne, 2013). Nevertheless, any attempt to fill the gap left by NPM is only sustainable if new institutional arrangements and new management styles are put in place; that is, in order for co-creation to be prolific, it has to be instantiated by systemic changes.

Although allegedly outdated (Drechsler, 2005; Levy, 2010; Lynn, 1998), the strategies promoted by NPM can be still observed in practice and tend to hamper the creation of an arena propitious to co-creation. Outcome management through performance-based policies has led to increasing standardisation and bureaucratisation of public administration (Moynihan, 2013) and, as explained in the previous sections, has promoted rebellious behaviours among front-line workers who perceive it as an attempt to control their practice and limit ability to innovate (Rocha & Holmen, 2020). This ultimately has reduced productivity (Jacobsen et al., 2014; Røiseland et al., 2015). Likewise, the profits from outsourcing public services to private sector service providers are not as high as imagined, and they tend to be outweighed by transaction and management costs (Petersen et al., 2018). The concern is now not to return to the times of public bureaucracy and specify better how co-creation fits in the post-NPM era we have been experiencing (Drechsler, 2005; Du Gay, 2000; Pollitt & Bouckaert, 2004).

The notion of co-creation, in this book suggested to be deployed with the help of tools and strategies provided by activity theory, emphasises collaborative relationships between both public, private and third-sector organisations as well as service users. These interactions tend to be ultimately reified by front-line workers, especially at the local level, where there is a pressing need to gather resources to counterbalance the cross-pressure between increasing challenges and expectations and the paucity of funds (Torfing et al., 2019), not to mention the complex demands in today's society that nearly mandate interagency collaboration in order for service users' needs to be met, which justifies the inclusion of their perspective as much as possible in the process of innovation (Lusch & Vargo, 2006).

The mounting critique of NPM has led to the search for alternatives. Co-creation in the public sector appears an attractive means to offset the perils provoked by years of NPM. Emphasis on the exchange of knowledge, resources and competences between the public, private and third sectors and service users should increase the production of value concerning visions, policies, strategies or services (Torfing et al., 2019). The challenge, however, has been to find ways to overcome the political resistance accruing from new institutional designs and new forms of public leadership. In the next chapters, the use of the tools and strategies provided by activity theory is suggested as an accessible means to tackle political and institutional resistance, as they help to put in practice the notions that otherwise are just on the book pages.

1.3 References

Andrews, D., & Bonta, J. (2016). *The psychology of criminal conduct*. Routledge.

Armstrong, S., & McNeill, F. (2012). London. *Reducing reoffending: Review of selected countries*. Edinburgh: The Scottish Centre for Crime and Justice Research.

Atkinson, M., Jones, M., & Lamont, E. (2007). *Multi-agency working and its implications for practice: A review of the literature*. Reading: CFBT Education Trust.

Bond, B., & Gittell, J. (2010). Cross-agency coordination of offender reentry: Testing collaboration outcomes. *Journal of Criminal Justice*, 38, pp. 118–129. Doi: 10.1016/j.jcrimjus.2010.02.003.

Boscarato, K., Lee, S., Kroschel, J., Hollander, Y., Brennan, A., & Warren, N. (2014). Consumer experience of formal crisis-response services and preferred methods of crisis intervention. *International Journal of Mental Health Nursing*, 23(4), pp. 287–295. Doi: 10.1111/inm.12059.

Bradley, K. (2009). *The Bradley report: Lord Bradley's review of people with mental health problems or learning disabilities in the criminal justice system* (Vol. 7). London: Department of Health.

Carter, P. R. Baron Carter of Coles. (2007). *Securing the future: Proposals for the efficient and sustainable use of custody in England and Wales*. London: Home Office.

Clarke, B. (2013). Practice values versus contract values: The importance of a culture of reflective practice. *British Journal of Community Justice*, (2–3), pp. 109–114.

Clayfield, J. C., Grudzinskas, J. A. J., Fisher, W. H., & Roy-Bujnowski, K. (2005). E pluribus unum: Creating a multi-organizational structure for serving arrestees with serious mental illness. *Research in Social Problems & Public Policy*, 12, pp. 27–49. Doi: 10.1016/S0196-1152(05)12002-X.

Department i Helse og Omsorg. (2013). *Morgendagens omsorg: Norwegian government white paper no. 29*. Oslo: Helse og Omsorg Department.

Department of Health. (2010). *Equity and excellence: Liberating the NHS*. London: Department of Health.

Department of Health. (2013). *Statement of government policy on adult safeguarding*. London: Department of Health and Social Care.

Department of Health and Concordat Signatories. (2014). *Improving outcomes for people experiencing mental health crisis*. London: HM Government.

Drechsler, W. (2005). The rise and demise of the new public management. *Post-Autistic Economics Review*, 33(14), pp. 17–28. Doi: 10.17573/cepar.v7i3.131.

Du Gay, P. (2000). *In praise of bureaucracy*. London, England: SAGE.

Earl, F., Cocksedge, K., Rheeder, B., Morgan, J., & Palmer, J. (2015). Neighbourhood outreach: A novel approach to liaison and diversion. *The Journal of Forensic Psychiatry & Psychology*, 26(5), pp. 573–585. Doi: 10.1080/14789949.2015.1045428.

Ellis, K. (2007). Direct payments and social work practice: The significance of "street-level bureaucracy" in determining eligibility. *British Journal of Social Work*, 37, pp. 405–422. Doi: 10.1093/bjsw/bcm013.

Fazel, S., & Danesh, J. (2002). Serious mental disorder in 23 000 prisoners: A systematic review of 62 surveys. *The Lancet*, 359(9306), pp. 545–550. Doi: 10.1016/S0140-6736(02)07740-1.

Fazel, S., & Wolf, A. (2015). A systematic review of criminal recidivism rates worldwide: Current difficulties and recommendations for best practice. *PLoS ONE*, 10(6). Doi: 10.1371/journal.pone.0130390.

Fenge, L.-A., Hean, S., Staddon, S., Clapper, A., Heaslip, V., & Jack, E. (2014). Mental health and the criminal justice system: The role of interagency training to promote practitioner understanding of the diversion agenda. *Journal of Social Welfare and Family Law*, 36(1), pp. 36–46. Doi: 10.1080/09649069.2014.891338.

Fuglsang, L. (2010). Bricolage and invisible innovation in the public service innovation. *Journal of Innovation Economics*, (1), pp. 67–87. Doi: 10.3917/jie.005.0067.

Frost, N. (2005). *Professionalism, partnership and joined-up thinking: A research review of front-line working with children and families*. Sheffield: Research in practice.

Great Britain Home Office. (2015). *Alternative place of safety: The West Sussex pilot evaluation 2015*. London: Great Britain: Home Office.

Hean, S., Warr, J., & Staddon, S. (2009). Challenges at the interface of working between mental health services and criminal justice system. *Medicine, Science and the Law*, 49, pp. 170–178. Doi: 10.1258/rsmmsl.49.3.170.

Herbst, M. (2007). *Financing public universities*. Dordrecht: Springer Netherlands.

Herrington, V., Clifford, K., Lawrence, P., Ryle, S., & Pope, R. (2009). *The impact of the NSW police force mental health intervention team: Final evaluation report*. New South Wales: Charles Sturt University.

Hill, M., & Huppe, P. (2014). *Implementing public policy: An introduction to the study of operational governance*. London: Sage.

Home Office. (2015). *Supporting vulnerable people who encounter the police: A strategic guide for police forces and their partners*. London: Home Office.

Home Office Department of Health. (2000). *No secrets: Guidance on developing and implementing multi-agency policies and procedures to protect vulnerable adults from abuse*. London: Home Office Department of Health.

Home Office UK. (2014). *Multi-agency working and information sharing project: Final report*. London: Home Office.

Hood, C., & Dixon, R. (2015). *A government that worked better and cost less?* Oxford, UK: Oxford University Press.

Hupe, P. (2014). What happens on the ground: Persistent issues in implementation research. *Public Policy and Administration*, 29(2), pp. 164–182. Doi: 10.1177/0952076713518339.

Hupe, P., & Hill, M. (2016). "And the rest is implementation": Comparing approaches to what happens in policy processes beyond great expectations. *Public Policy and Administration*, 31(2), p. 103. Doi: 10.1177/0952076715598828.

Jacobsen, C. B., Hvitved, J., & Andersen, L. B. (2014). Command and motivation: How the perception of external interventions relates to intrinsic motivation and public service motivation. *Public Administration*, 92, pp. 790–806. Doi: 10.1111/padm.12024.

James, D. (1999). Court diversion at 10 years: Can it work, does it work and has it a future? *The Journal of Forensic Psychiatry*, 10(3), pp. 507–524. Doi: 10.1080/09585189908402156.

James, D., Kerrigan, T., Forfar, R., Franham, F., & Preston, L. (2010). The Fixated Threat Assessment Centre: Preventing harm and facilitating care. *The Journal of Forensic Psychiatry & Psychology*, 21(4), pp. 521–536. Doi: 10.1080/14789941003596981.

Jenkins, K. (2014). *Information-sharing in mental health care provision: A review.*

Kodner, D., & Spreeuwenberg, C. (2002). Integrated care: Meaning, logic, applications, and implications: A discussion paper. *International Journal of Integrated Care*, 2(4). Doi: 10.5334/ijic.67.

Laign, R., Halsey, R., Donohue, D., & Cashin, A. (2009). Application of a model for the development of a mental health service delivery collaboration between police and the health service. *Issues in Mental Health Nursing*, 30(5), pp. 337–341. Doi: 10.1080/01612840902754644.

Levy, R. (2010). New public management: End of an era? *Public Administration Review*, 25, pp. 234–240. Doi: 10.1177/0952076709357152.

Lippke, L., & Wegener, C. (2014). Everyday innovation: Pushing boundaries while maintaining stability. *Journal of Workplace Learning*, 26(6–7), pp. 376–391. Doi: 10.1108/JWL-10-2013-0086.

Lipsky, M. (2010). *Street-level bureaucracy: Dilemmas of the individual in public services. 30th Anniversary expanded edition.* New York: Russell Sage.

Lusch, R. P., & Vargo, S. L. (Eds.). (2006). *The service-dominant logic of marketing: Dialogue, debate, and directions.* Armonk, NY: Scharpe.

Lynn, L. E. (1998). The new public management: How to transform a theme into a legacy. *Public Administration Review*, 58, pp. 231–237. Doi: 10.1177/0020852301672009.

Maynard-Moody, S., & Musheno, M. (2003). *Cops, teachers, counselors: Stories from the front lines of public service.* Ann Arbor: University of Michigan Press.

McGilloway, S., & Donnelly, M. (2004). Mental illness in the UK criminal justice system: A police liaison scheme for mentally disordered offenders in Belfast. *Journal of Mental Health*, 13, pp. 263–275. Doi: 10.1080/09638230410001700899.

Ministry of Justice UK. (2013). *Transforming rehabilitation: A revolution in the way we manage offenders.* London: The Stationery Office.

Moynihan, D. P. (2013). Advancing the empirical study of performance management. *The American Review of Public Administration*, 43, pp. 499–517. Doi: 10.1177/0275074013487023.

NHS England Liaison and Diversion Programme. (2014). *Liaison and diversion operation model 2013/14*. London: The NHS Constitution. Retrieved from www. england.nhs.uk/wp-content/uploads/2014/04/ld-op-mod-1314.pdf

Oliver, C., Mooney, A., & Statham, J. (2010). *Integrated working: A review of the evidence*. London: University of London.

Parker, A., Scantlebury, A., Booth, A., MacBryde, J., Scott, W., Wright, K., & McDaid, C. (2018). Interagency collaboration models for people with mental ill health in contact with the police: A systematic scoping review. *BMJ Open*, 8. Doi: 10.1136/bmjopen-2017-019312.

Petersen, O. H., Hjelmar, U., & Vrangbæk, K. (2018). Is contracting out of public services still the great panacea? A systematic review of studies on economic and quality effects from 2000 to 2014. *Social Policy & Administration*, 52(1), pp. 130–157. Doi: 10.1111/spol.12297.

Phillips, C., Considine, M., & Lewis, R. (2000). *A review of audits and strategies produced by crime and disorder partnerships in 1999: Briefing note*. London: Home Office, Research, Development and Statistics Directorate, Policing and Reducing Crime Unit.

Pollitt, C., & Bouckaert, G. (2004). *Public management reform: A comparative analysis*. Oxford, UK: Oxford University Press.

Radnor, Z., & Osborne, S. P. (2013). Lean: A failed theory for public services? *Public Management Review*, 15, pp. 265–287. Doi: 10.1080/14719037.2012. 748820.

Reed, J. (1992). *Review of health and social services for mentally disordered offenders and those requiring similar services*. Department of Health/Home Office. London: HMSO.

Rocha, P., & Holmen, A. (2020). Performance-based policy in offender rehabilitation: Limitation or innovation for front-line workers in liaison and diversion services? *Probation Journal*. Doi: 10.1177/0264550520926578.

Røiseland, A., Pierre, J., & Gustavsen, A. (2015). Accountability by professionalism or managerialism? Exploring attitudes among Swedish and Norwegian local government leaders. *International Journal of Public Administration*, 38, pp. 689–700. Doi: 10.1080/01900692.2014.955196.

Sainsbury Centre for Mental Health. (2009). *Diversion: A better way for criminal justice and mental health*. London: Nuffield Press.

Sinha, S. (2010). Adjustment and mental health problem in prisoners. *Industrial Psychiatry Journal*, 19(2), pp. 101–104. Doi: 10.4103/0972-6748.90339.

Statham, J. (2011). *A review of international evidence on interagency working, to inform the development of Children's Services Committees in Ireland*. Dublin: Department of Children and Youth Affairs.

Strype, J., Gundhus, H., Egge, M., & Ødegård, A. (2014). Perceptions of interprofessional collaboration. *Profession and Professionalism*, 4(3), p. 806. Doi: 10.7577/pp.806.

Torfing, J., Sørensen, E., & Røiseland, A. (2019). Transforming the public sector into an arena for co-creation: Barriers, drivers, benefits, and ways forward. *Administration & Society*, 51(5), pp. 795–825. Doi: 10.1177/009539971 6680057.

UK Crown. (2007). *Mental health act 2007*. London: The Stationery Office.

Williams, I. (2009). Offender Health and Social Care: A Review of the Evidence on Inter-Agency Collaboration. *Health and Social Care in the Community* (6), pp. 573-580. Doi: 10.1111/j.1365-2524.2009.00857.

Williams, P. (2012). *Collaboration in policy and practice: Perspectives on boundary spanners*. Bristol: Public Policy Press.

Winters, S., Magalhaes, L., & Kinsella, E. (2015). Interprofessional collaboration in mental health crisis response systems: A scoping review. *Disabil Rehabil*, 37, pp. 2212–2224. Doi: 10.3109/09638288.2014.1002576.

World Health Organization. (2015). *WHO global strategy on people-centred and integrated health services: Interim report (No. WHO/HIS/SDS/2015.6)*. Geneva, Switzerland: World Health Organization.

World Health Organization. (2005). *Mental health: Facing the challenges, building solutions: Report from the WHO European Ministerial Conference*. Geneva, Switzerland: WHO Regional Office Europe.

2 Theoretical framework

Activity theory and innovation in the public sector

This chapter introduces the theoretical framework underpinning the study reported herein. The empirical work (see Chapter 3 in this book) reflected upon in this book was based on cultural-historical activity theory (CHAT) combined with the notion of innovation reified through front-line workers in the public-sector services. The use of CHAT and street-level innovation to make sense of collaborative practice at the street level engenders a holistic framework designed to avoid heuristics and bootstrapping, promising creative discussions on intricate issues that disrupt good practice.

2.1 Activity theory

Activity theory is an umbrella term that includes various theories addressing the developmental processes of practical social activities (Sannino et al., 2009). It originated in the Soviet Union but has been rather popular in the West since the 1970s in the fields of education and information systems. It is grounded in three basic principles across an array of interpretations and adaptations of the theory, as follows: 1) every activity is object oriented (Foot, 2001), 2) artefacts and tools mediate the relationship between the subject and object and 3) contradictions prompt developmental expansion cycles within and between activity systems (Engeström, 1987).

Activity theory resorts to triangular models to depict the mediated relationship between "subject" and "object" in any given activity. In its third generation (to learn more about activity theory's generations, see Engeström, 1987), the triangular model is expanded to also take into account the influence of elements such as "rules," "community" and "division of labour" on the subject-object relationship, as depicted in Figure 2.1. Thus, the main contribution of the third generation of activity theory (also known as cultural-historical activity theory) is to analyse multiple activity systems simultaneously (Engeström, 2001). In the offender rehabilitation context, these systems might be two adjacent services that have common

DOI: 10.4324/9781003186793-2

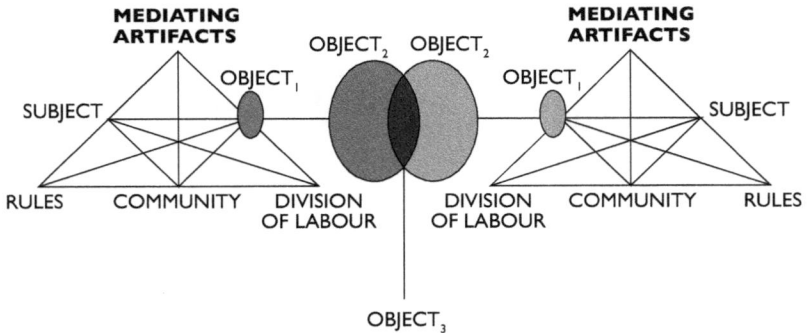

Figure 2.1 Representation of a minimal unity of analysis in the third generation of CHAT

Source: (Engeström, 2001).

goals working together, for example, the police custody officers collaborating with liaison and diversion workers to screen, assess and divert vulnerable individuals when they enter the criminal justice system.

There is a lot written about activity theory in the scientific literature. In this book, the exploration of the theory is bound by the existent street-level circumstances that limit collaborative practice across the criminal justice and welfare systems. In other words, the emphasis herein is on the notion of "contradictions" and how their resolution can lead to innovation in the public sector. A more detailed study of activity theory is, therefore, beyond the scope of this book but can be found elsewhere (Engeström, 1987; Foot, 2001; Kerosuo et al., 2010; Rocha, 2020; Sannino et al., 2009).

Tensions within an element of an activity system, between the elements of an activity system or even between elements of different activity systems create challenges (or contradictions). Consequently, the subject of the activity might be impaired in achieving its goal (or object) and the pursued outcome. These contradictions can be interpreted as "sources of change and development" (Engeström, 2001, p. 137), as they can potentially start systemic transformation through a process of "expansive learning" (Engeström, 2001).

2.1.1 Activity systems, contradictions and expansive learning

In cultural-historical activity theory, consciousness does not exist in abstract. It is bequeathed to the individual through activity (Vygotsky, 1987). Thus, human beings cannot be analysed as separate entities but only as part of an activity, which transforms individuals and activities into a unity of analysis (Engeström, 1987). Activity systems, then, are used to represent collaborative relations between people in object-oriented activities mediated by tools, division of labour and rules (Ploettner & Tresseras, 2016). In this book, the object of the activity of criminal justice workers, for instance, is the enforcement of the law and protection of the community, while the object of the activity of welfare services professionals is to ensure the welfare of patients.

However, activity systems are not impervious units. They are constantly affected by other activities and other changes in their environment. These external factors can create imbalances in the elements of an activity. In CHAT, the term "contradiction" is adopted to represent a tension that can happen either within the elements of an activity system (primary-level contradiction), between the elements of an activity system (secondary-level contradiction), between different developmental phases of a single activity (tertiary-level contradiction) or between different activity systems (quaternary-level contradictions). Contradictions are development igniters, as activities are virtually always in the process of working through contradictions and creating new improved activities (for more on the four levels of contradictions, see, e.g., Engeström, 1987; Foot, 2014; Rocha, 2020).

Since in CHAT the combination of multiple activity systems is considered the unit of analysis (Engeström, 2001), contradictions tend to be structural tensions within and between these systems. In the case example of this book, potential contradictions within and between the activity systems of both the criminal justice and welfare services function as igniters to expansive learning cycles that ultimately lead to transformation across all the interrelated activity systems and potentially innovation in the public sector.

The expansive learning cycle is the process whereby the resolution of existent contradictions in the current activity system happens. It promotes mutual learning, leading to a new activity with a novel shared object (Kerosuo et al., 2010). Generally, it starts with the emergence of a state of need in an activity. The need state is the initial phase in which the subjects question the activity in which they are participating. In a second moment, the initial tension existent within an element of the activity system tends to reverberate across all the others. To move forward, an analysis of the reasons behind the existent contradictions is necessary. The result of such an analysis should be a breakthrough that engenders the modelling of new solutions for the activity. New solutions include, for example, the development of a new object or new instruments for the activity. Once new solutions are modelled, they should be examined and tested to ensure effectiveness. Only then, after necessary adjustments are made, should a new model emerge. Finally, the new model should be implemented in replacement of the current one. However, during the implementation, new contradictions can occur between the current and the new models, for example, employees can resist the use of new instruments. Therefore, the implementation process should be instantiated by reflections on the expansive learning cycle as a whole and its consequences in order to consolidate any new practice. A graphic representation of this stepwise process can be found in Figure 2.2.

It is important to bear in mind that the expansive learning cycle is a heuristic device. It describes the ideal scenario in which all the necessary steps to the resolution of contradictions are carried out. In practice, however, they hardly are. What is important to understand is that the expansive learning cycle represents a process of construction and resolution of successively evolving contradictions (Engeström & Sannino, 2010). It is through the resolution of contradictions that transformation emerges, and every change in the status quo is a form of innovation.

The activity-theoretical notion of expansive learning cycle dovetails nicely with the notion of innovation espoused in this book, that is, that it emerges organically from practice as an incremental process corollary of the cumulative learning process where new ideas build upon the ones that already exist, which is an understanding widely supported in the literature (Fuglsang & Sørensen, 2011; Gallouj & Weinstein, 1997; Sundbo, 1997; Styhre, 2009; Toivonen & Tuominen, 2009; Van de Ven et al., 2008).

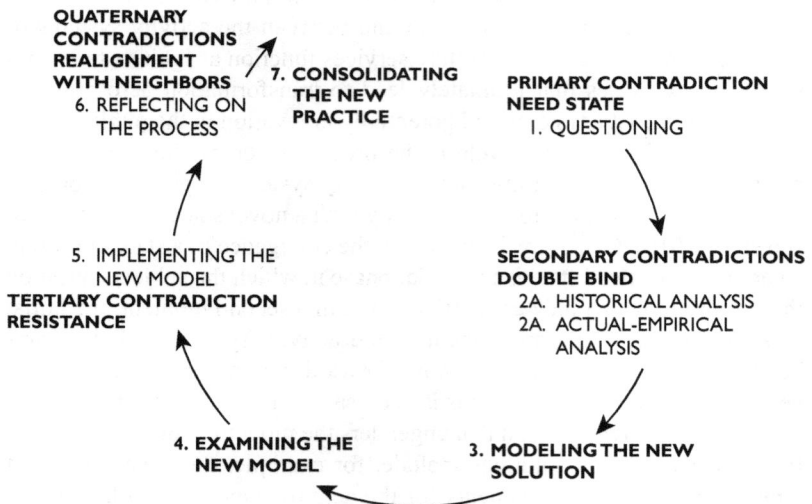

QUATERNARY
CONTRADICTIONS
REALIGNMENT
WITH NEIGHBORS   7. CONSOLIDATING   PRIMARY CONTRADICTION
6. REFLECTING ON   THE NEW   NEED STATE
   THE PROCESS   PRACTICE   I. QUESTIONING

5. IMPLEMENTING THE   SECONDARY CONTRADICTIONS
   NEW MODEL   DOUBLE BIND
TERTIARY CONTRADICTION   2A. HISTORICAL ANALYSIS
RESISTANCE   2A. ACTUAL-EMPIRICAL
                                               ANALYSIS

4. EXAMINING THE   3. MODELING THE NEW
   NEW MODEL   SOLUTION

Figure 2.2 Expansive learning cycle
Source: (Engeström, 2001).

As mentioned in Chapter 1, there is a need for effective models of collaboration at the interface between the criminal justice and welfare systems (Fenge et al., 2014). Innovative strategies to tackle the challenges of a rapidly changing workplace environment make a case for the espousal of a theory capable of making sense of interagency collaboration in the context. Although CHAT has been used successfully and extensively in the research of organisational settings in a range of contexts, for example, organisational studies (Blackler & Regan, 2009), human resource development and management practices (Gvaramadze, 2008) and organisational and individual learning (Engeström et al., 2007), its adoption in the offender rehabilitation setting is still an underexplored idea, with little research done on the challenges of front-line interagency collaboration between criminal justice and welfare services.

At the interface between criminal justice and welfare systems, working is challenging because of the clash between two distinctive cultures, namely a focus on security issues versus an emphasis on health and social care outcomes (Fenge et al., 2014). In this melting pot, the chances of tensions occurring between activity systems are high. A setting with existent contradiction is perfect for innovation attained through cycles of expansive learning. Thus, the use of CHAT in the offender rehabilitation setting is, although innovative, germane and productive.

2.1.2 The change laboratory model

There is a proclivity for innovation in the public sector to be initiated by central levels of the government in a top-down manner, such as the liaison and diversion services national model. This approach is predicated on the assumption that standardised instructions can be equally applied across diverse contexts (Lipsky, 2010). However, one-size-fits-all models have already been contested elsewhere (Rittel & Webber, 1973; Rocha & Holmen, 2020), as the effectiveness of any solution is strongly dependent on its context.

Although this book draws upon the findings of a case study on L&D services, the evidence produced seems to represent a sub-species of a broader genre already addressed in the scientific literature, namely the need for collaboration between actors interested in innovation in the public sector (Ellström, 2010; Fuglsang, 2010; Hill & Huppe, 2014; Høyrup, 2010; Lipsky, 2010). The procedures carried out by the several L&D sites across England are the reflection of their local contexts and are deeply embedded in their work routines. Therefore, any attempt to innovate needs first to take into account the cultural and historical circumstances of each L&D site and only then break away from previous practices.

CHAT champions that collaboration and innovation are matters to be addressed bottom-up. Thus, policymakers and decision-makers should support employee-driven innovation processes and create an appropriate environment where open dialogue between actors at different strata is attainable. To that end, future research should look into alternatives that do not rely on top-down initiatives but instead emphasise the resourcefulness of frontline professionals in initiating solutions. On that note, the change laboratory model (CLM) is a tool to promote innovation and learning within and between organisations. It draws upon activity-theoretical concepts, and it provides those interested with a toolkit appropriate to tackle the challenge of innovatively promoting integrated care in a fragmented setting (Kerosuo & Engeström, 2003; Tolviainen, 2007). Its adequacy has been put to the test in various interagency workplaces (Kerosuo & Engeström, 2003; Querol et al., 2014; Tolviainen, 2007), and the outcomes confirm the benefits of co-devised solutions.

Traditionally, the CLM makes use of wallboards to represent the participants' work activity. The horizontal dimensions of the wallboards depict different levels of abstraction and generalisation, whereas the vertical dimensions represent the change in time (past, present and future). In the mirror wallboard, daily work practices are gathered, for example, videotaped episodes of work, interviews and stories. In the model/vision wallboard, activity-theoretical concepts help with the analysis of the data from the mirror wallboard. Finally, in the ideas/tools wallboard, participants find the resources created during the sessions, that is, intermediate cognitive tools such as schedules, schemes and charts (Engeström & Escalante, 1996). Figure 2.3 illustrates the CLM basic setting.

The CLM is kicked off with participants analysing current contradictions in an activity. The aim is to find the origins of existing tensions by modelling previous iterations of the activity. The next step is to model current activity as well, including its contradictions. Then participants design a future model and develop a plan to achieve it. The entire process takes several sessions and lasts from three to six months (Engeström & Escalante, 1996). In the end, new alternatives are created with the expansion of the activity's objects; the development of new tools, rules or communities; or even the redesign of the division of labour (Engeström et al., 2007).

In the context of offender rehabilitation, while current collaborative practices such as care pathways and care plans endeavour to standardise practice as opposed to providing customised solutions, the CLM could be adopted as a means to reify innovation bottom-up. The CLM would allow professionals to work in tandem to resolve issues they have identified as problematic rather than having to comply with standardised solutions imposed

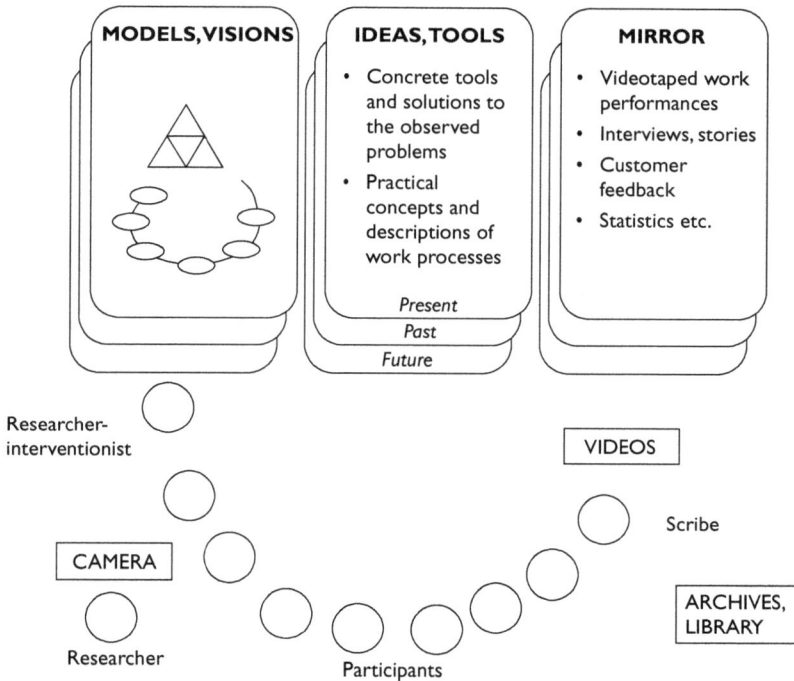

Figure 2.3 Basic setup for CLM
Source: (Adapted from Engeström, 1987).

top-down, something that has already been shown to be ineffective (Rittel & Webber, 1973).

2.2 Innovation in the public sector: interagency collaboration in the public sector

Along general lines, innovation entails the development and implementation of something new (de Jong & Vermeulen, 2003), or at least the combination of existing ideas and resources in a novel way (Schumpeter, 1934). There is a stream of literature that conceptualises innovation as a generic three-phased process: first the generation of an idea, then its development and finally its implementation (Booz et al., 1982), sort of a defined planned project (Van de Ven et al., 2008). However, this book espouses the understanding that innovation might also organically emerge from practice. This notion finds grounding in organisational settings, where often the development of new ideas is intertwined with mundane processes of the company (Sundbo, 1997; Toivonen & Tuominen, 2009), such as in the cases of ad hoc innovation (Gallouj & Weinstein, 1997), tinkering (Styhre, 2009) and bricolage (Fuglsang & Sørensen, 2011). Shared by these approaches is the notion that new ideas might result from workers' creative thinking to meet the customers' needs (ad hoc innovation), that innovation can represent a leeway to adjust a protocol to unexpected events (tinkering) or that innovation can also be a planned move initiated at the street level to address a problem (bricolage).

This book champions not only that innovation can emerge from practice but also that it can be an incremental process corollary of cumulative learning processes where new ideas build upon others that already existed (Fuglsang & Sørensen, 2011; Van de Ven et al., 2008). This allows for a concept of innovation that is intertwined with practice also to include improvement consequent of regular learning activities (Fuglsang & Sørensen, 2011; Gallouj & Weinstein, 1997; Sundbo, 1997; Van de Ven et al., 2008).

2.2.1 Service innovation processes: top-down versus bottom-up perspectives

Traditionally, public-sector innovation has been initiated via top-down processes driven by political decisions (Walker, 2006) that called for standard injunctions being equally implemented by front-line professionals across settings despite local circumstances (Lipsky, 2010). In the late 1980s and early 1990s, innovation processes to improve public sector efficiency mostly followed the new public management agenda, especially in countries such as the UK and USA. NPM was usually characterised by a series of reforms and restructures to make the public services more "business-like" and to improve their efficiency through private-sector management models, for example, to divide large public bureaucracies to create less hierarchical organisations, to increase competition by introducing private-sector service providers in the realm of public services and to drive outcome through performance-based policies that remunerated good performance (Keen, 2010).

The use of a performance-based approach in public policymaking and management allegedly increases accountability of governments and facilitates performance assessment, as it enables a clear articulation of the problem addressed by the policy and how the government should intervene, a clear identification of the policy expected outcomes, the development of an independent assessment plan for the implementation, the enforcement and outcomes of the policy and the development of an evaluation plan for identification of success/failure factors to inform future policymaking (Bouckaert & Halligan, 2008; Fryer et al., 2009; Kuhlman, 2010; van Dooren et al., 2010). Performance-based policing was an important strategy supporting the NPM agenda, but its use can still be noticed today to a certain degree (Rocha & Holmen, 2020).

In the UK, for example, the NPM agenda has gained relevance again with the 2010 UK election of a coalition government that shared enthusiasm for the mixed economy of public service provision (Albertson et al., 2018). Top-down, performance-based policymaking has become popular in different areas of government, including welfare-to-work programmes, public health budgets and the criminal justice system (Bochel & Powell, 2016). An example of the approach is the national model for liaison and diversion services that links funding to the ability the service has to achieve the outcomes specified in the policy (NHS England Liaison and Diversion Programme, 2014). However, there seems to be an inherent clash between the NPM approach and the notion of innovation, as the latter requires experimentation, while the former prioritises the reward of success. Consequently, risk-averse front-line workers must focus on fail-proof initiatives that have been tested in the past rather than experimenting with new service designs, which ultimately deters innovation (McGahey & Willis, 2017).

An alternative to the top-down, performance-based approach to innovation that has gained increased adherence in recent years is the bottom-up, practice-based approach to innovation where employees and their workplace make up an arena for learning and innovation (Kesting & Ulhøi, 2010). Central to the bottom-up, practice-based innovation strategy is the acceptance that novelty can be an outcome of the work practice and the employees' reflective experiences, which links innovation with learning experiences taking place at street-level practice. In other words, by having employees renewing working methods, routines, products and services, innovation becomes a natural corollary of their learning processes (Ellström, 2010).

In a bottom-up practice-based approach, communities of practice serve as a site for employees to innovate through work (Brown & Duguid, 2001; Wenger, 2000). A community of practice is a group of professionals who share similar interests and cultural practices, for example, police officers in custody, mental health practitioners in a hospital and liaison and diversion workers in a specific L&D site. In an environment where everyone shares similar work practice, collective learning is more easily achieved, resulting in the production of new knowledge. Another characteristic of a community of practice is that it serves as an arena for the development, maintenance and reproduction of the very knowledge that is produced within it (Brown & Duguid, 1991).

In this new paradigm, it is the front-line workers' responsibility to promote innovation in public sector organisations (Arundel & Huber, 2013). As top-down policies often do meet citizens' demands (Hartley, 2005), deviations from their injunctions promote an organic transformation initiated at the front line. Once transformation spreads and develops into a routinised way of performing the work, it becomes the new work practice. Thus, practice-based innovation can be perceived as a cyclical process of learning, whereby deviation from previous work routines initiates a learning process that develops into new work practice (Ellström, 2010), rather similar to the steps comprising an expansive learning cycle, as described in Section 2.1.1.

In contrast with the top-down, management-initiated approach to innovation where front-line workers merely implement new policy at the street level, the bottom-up, practice-based approach empowers employees. Either way, both approaches require communication and coordination between all those involved in the process. If managers feel that practice-based solutions are threatening the order of the system, they will most likely not support them (Høyrup, 2010). Likewise, an attempt to innovate coming from management might also fail if front-line workers do not recognise it as relevant at the street level (Lipsky, 2010).

In sum, effective innovation processes require both strategic directions for innovation that are initiated top down along with the presence of ideas emerging throughout the organisation in a bottom-up fashion (Fuglsang & Sundbo, 2005; Sundbo & Fuglsang, 2002). That is where adopting cultural-historical activity theory becomes advantageous, as it provides a set of instruments to study transformations and social processes of innovation and make sense of them through cycles of expansive learning.

2.3 The need for a new approach to public service delivery

Contemporary public management theory is still strongly influenced by the new public management premise (Hood, 1991) of public officials being a self-serving elite that only looks after its own interests (Cole & Caputo, 1984), which renders public administration an inefficient and ineffective means to allocate public resources (Osborne & Gaebler, 1993). Consequently, a pointedly managerial approach to public service delivery is still generally perceived in the public sector through, for example, the rendition of services as basic units and a consequent focus on their costs, the focus of performance management and output control and the interpretation of citizens as customers (Osborne, 2010).

This book, however, debates the adequacy of the managerial (instead of administrative/professional) approach for public services (Hood & Jackson, 1991; Pollitt & Bouckaert, 2000; Thomas, 2012). Although the question of efficient use of public resources has always been around, in the current state of fragmentation of the state (Haveri, 2006), the intraorganisational focus of the NPM paradigms do not meet the interorganisational nature of contemporary services delivery in the public sector. Therefore, new models have appeared to attempt to respond to this new scenario, for example, including public value (Moore, 2002), digital governance (Dunleavy et al., 2006) and the new public governance (Osborne, 2010).

More important than any specific model, it is crucial to take a holistic and systemic approach to the delivery of public services, an approach that recognises and responds to the external, interorganisational scenario of contemporary public management. This can only happen if service user expectations and experiences occupy central roles. Citizens are essential stakeholders of the public policy and public service delivery processes, and their engagement is key. It is only through such an approach that sustainable models of service delivery in the public sector can thrive rather than attempts to re-enact public services as manufactured goods to be marketed in a managerial fashion.

Nevertheless, such a model would not come without challenges. A service-dominant approach to public management can be difficult to implement due to multiple and conflicting agendas amid those interested. In the case of the criminal justice system, for example, the definition of who the service user is in reality (the offender, the workers, the victims of crime, the society as a whole) is controversial (Bovaird, 2005). Activity theory provides tools to negotiate conflict situations such as this one, which renders it highly appropriate to the support of an innovative way to deliver public services. By placing the contradictions emerging from the interorganisational nature of contemporary service delivery in the public sector in a framework based upon activity theoretical principles, one can enrich their theoretical and practical understanding of public management as well as benefiting from tools that enable them to actually impact practice. What is necessary now is an agenda of empirical research to test out the insights and limitations of activity theory at the street level of the public service.

This book aims to contribute by using activity theory to address the perspective of front-line workers on interagency collaboration across criminal justice and welfare systems. In order to investigate the role of liaison and diversion as a bridge between services, two issues were investigated: first, how members of the L&D services perceived their role as facilitators of interagency collaboration across criminal justice and welfare systems in light of the standardised guidelines introduced by the new national model and, second, what the main contradictions found by L&D front-line workers were when trying to collaborate with neighbouring services to improve health and social care outcomes. The clarification of these issues was pivotal to the examination of the boundaries and overlaps between service users and service providers, the exploration of the impact of imposed policy on practice at the street level and the analysis of the impact of digital technology upon public service.

Although there is a great deal of research done on policy implementation at the street level as well as the consequences of discretionary street-level bureaucracy (Goldman & Foldy, 2015; Hill & Huppe, 2014; Lipsky, 2010; Rice, 2013), the perspective of front-line workers is still underexplored, especially the influence other actors have on the decision-making process carried out by front-line professionals. In the context of offender rehabilitation, the studies that do acknowledge interagency collaboration are to a great extent focused on the managerial point of view (Fenge et al., 2014; Hean et al., 2017; Kane et al., 2017).

Integrated care has been promoted as a means to decrease criminality (Fenge et al., 2014; Hean et al., 2009), but organisations' agendas tend to diverge. Consequently, constructing integrated care pathways to divert vulnerable offenders from the criminal justice system has become a challenge. The purpose of adopting activity theory to make sense of the described scenario is that the theory interprets such a challenge as an opportunity for organisational and interorganisational learning achieved through expansive cycles. The learning leads to innovation of existing work routines as well as the creation of new sorts of tools that ultimately take the object and forms of collaboration into consideration (De Dreu, 1997).

2.4 References

Albertson, K., Fox, C., O'Learly, C., Painter, G., Bailey, K., & Labarbera, J. (2018). *Payment by results and social impact bonds: Outcome-based payment systems in the UK and US.* Bristol: Policy Press Shorts Research. Doi: 10.2307/j.ctt21h4zbp.

Arundel, A., & Huber, D. (2013). From too little to too much innovation? Issues in monitoring innovation in the public sector. *Structural Change and Economic Dynamics*, 27, pp. 146–149. Doi: 10.1016/j.strueco.2013.06.009.

Blackler, F., & Regan, S. (2009). Intentionality, agency, change: Practice theory and management. *Management Learning*, 40(2), pp. 161–176. Doi: 10.1177/1350 507608101227.

Bochel, H., & Powell, M. (2016). The transformation of the welfare state? The Conservative-Liberal Democrat coalition government and social policy. In H. Bochel, & M. Powell, *The coalition government and social policy: Restructuring the welfare state* (pp. 1–25). Bristol: Policy Press. Doi: 10.1332/policypress/9781 447324560.003.0001.

Booz, A., & Hamilton. (1982). *New products management for the 1980s*. New York: Booz, Allen & Hamilton, Inc.

Bouckaert, G., & Halligan, J. (2008). *Managing performance: International comparisons*. London: Routledge. Doi: 10.4324/9780203935958.

Bovaird, T. (2005). Public governance: Balancing stakeholder power in a network society. *International Review of Administrative Sciences*, 71(2), pp. 217–228. Doi: 10.1177/0020852305053881.

Brown, J., & Duguid, P. (1991). Organizational learning and communities-of-practice: Toward a unified view of working, learning and innovation. *Organization Science*, 2(1), pp. 40–56.

Brown, J., & Duguid, P. (2001). Knowledge and organization: A social-practice perspective. *Organization Science*, 12(2), pp. 198–213. Doi: 10.1287/orsc.12.2. 198.10116.

Cole, R., & Caputo, D. (1984). The public hearing as an effective citizen participation mechanism: A case study of the general revenue sharing program. *American Political Science Review*, 78, pp. 404–416. Doi: 10.2307/1963372.

De Dreu, C. (1997). Productive conflict: The importance of conflict management and conflict issue. In C. De Dreu, & E. Van de Vliert, *Using Conflict in Organizations*. London: Sage Publications.

de Jong, J., & Vermeulen, P. (2003). Organizing successful new service development: A literature review. *Management Decision*, 41(9), pp. 844–858. Doi: 10.1108/00251740310491706.

Dunleavy, P., Margetts, H., Bastow, S., & Tinkler, J. (2006). New public management is dead: Long live digital-era governance. *Journal of Public Administration Research and Theory*, 16, pp. 467–494. Doi: 10.1093/jopart/mui057.

Ellström, P. (2010). Practice-based innovation: A learning perspective. *Journal of Workplace Learning*, 22(1–2), pp. 27–40. Doi: 10.1108/13665621011012834.

Engeström, Y. (1987). *Learning by expanding: An activity-theoretical approach to developmental research*. Helsinki: Orienta-Konsultit. Doi: 10.1017/CBO978 1139814744.

Engeström, Y. (2001). Learning at work: Toward an activity theoretical reconceptualization. *Journal of Education and Work*, (1), pp. 133–156. Doi: 10.1080/ 13639080123238.

Engeström, Y., & Escalante, V. (1996). Mundane tool or object of affection? The rise and fall of the postal buddy. In B. Nardi, *Context and consciousness: Activity theory and human computer interaction*. Cambridge, MA/London, England: The MIT Press.

Engeström, Y., Kerosuo, H., & Kajamaa, A. (2007). Beyond discontinuity expansive organizational learning remembered. *Management Learning*, 38(3), pp. 319–336. Doi: 10.1177/1350507607079032.

Engeström, Y., & Sannino, A. (2010). Studies of expansive learning: Foundations, findings and future challenges. *Educational Research Review*, 5(1), pp. 1–24. Doi: 10.1016/j.edurev.2009.12.002.

Fenge, L.-A., Hean, S., Staddon, S., Clapper, A., Heaslip, V., & Jack, E. (2014). Mental health and the criminal justice system: The role of interagency training to promote practitioner understanding of the diversion agenda. *Journal of Social Welfare and Family Law*, 36(1), pp. 36–46. Doi: 10.1080/09649069.2014.891338.

Foot, K. (2001). Cultural-historical activity theory as practice theory: Illuminating the development of conflict-monitoring network. *Communication Theory*, 11(1), pp. 56–83. Doi: 10.1111/j.1468-2885.2001.tb00233.x.

Foot, K. (2014). Cultural-historical activity theory: Exploring a theory to inform practice and research. *Journal of Human Behavior in the Social Environment,* 24(3), pp. 329–347. Doi: 10.1080/10911359.2013.831011.

Fryer, J., Antony, J., & Ogden, S. (2009). Performance management in the public sector. *International Journal of the Public Sector,* 22(6), pp. 478–498. Doi: 10.1108/09513550910982850.

Fuglsang, L. (2010). Bricolage and invisible innovation in the public service innovation. *Journal of Innovation Economics,* (1), pp. 67–87. Doi: 10.3917/jie.005.0067.

Fuglsang, L., & Sørensen, F. (2011). The balance between bricolage and innovation: Management dilemmas in sustainable public innovation. *Service Industries Journal,* 31(4), pp. 581–595. Doi: 10.1080/02642069.2010.504302.

Fuglsang, L., & Sundbo, J. (2005). The organizational innovation system: Three modes. *Journal of Change Management,* 5(3), pp. 329–344. Doi: 10.1080/146970 10500258056.

Gallouj, F., & Weinstein, O. (1997). Innovation in services. *Research Policy,* 26, pp. 537–556. Doi: 10.1016/S0048-7333(97)00030-9.

Goldman, L., & Foldy, E. (2015). The space before action: The role of peer discussion groups in frontline service provision. *Chicago Journals,* 89(1), pp. 166–202. Doi: 10.1086/680319.

Gvaramadze, I. (2008). Human resource development practice: The paradox of empowerment and individualization. *Human Resource Development International,* 11(5), pp. 465–477. Doi: 10.1080/13678860802417601.

Hartley, J. (2005). Innovation in governance and public services: Past and present. *Public Money Manage,* 25, pp. 27–34. Doi: 10.1111/j.1467-9302.2005.00447.x.

Haveri, A. (2006). Complexity in local government change. *Public Management Review,* 8(1), pp. 31–46. Doi: 10.1080/14719030500518667.

Hean, S., Ødegård, A., & Willumsen, E. (2017). Improving collaboration between professionals supporting mentally ill offenders. *International Journal of Prisoner Health,* 13(2), pp. 91–104. Doi: 10.1108/IJPH-12-2016-0072.

Hean, S., Warr, J., & Staddon, S. (2009). Challenges at the interface of working between mental health services and criminal justice system. *Medicine, Science and the Law,* 49, pp. 170–178. Doi: 10.1258/rsmmsl.49.3.170.

Hill, M., & Huppe, P. (2014). *Implementing public policy: An introduction to the study of operational governance.* London: Sage.

Hood, C. (1991). A public management for all seasons? *Public Administration,* 69, pp. 3–19. Doi: 10.1111/j.1467-9299.1991.tb00779.x.

Hood, C., & Jackson, M. (1991). The new public management: A recipe for disaster. *Canberra Bulletin of Public Administration,* pp. 16–24.

Høyrup, S. (2010). Employee-driven innovation and workplace learning: Basic concepts, approaches and themes. *Transfer,* 16, pp. 143–154. Doi: 10.1177/10242 58910364102.

Kane, E., Evans, E., & Shokraneh, F. (2017). Effectiveness of current policing-related mental health interventions: A systematic review. *Criminal Behaviour and Mental Health,* 28(2), pp. 108–119. Doi: 10.1002/cbm.2058.

Keen, J. (2010). Integration at any price: The case of the NHS national programme for information technology. In H. Margetts, Perri 6, & C. Hood, *Paradoxes of modernization: Unintended consequences of public policy reform* (pp. 138–154). Oxford: Oxford University Press. Doi: 10.1093/acprof:oso/9780199573547.003.0008.

Kerosuo, H., & Engeström, Y. (2003). Boundary crossing and learning in creation of new work practice. *Journal of Workplace Learning*, 15(7/8), pp. 345–351. Doi: 10.1108/13665620310504837.

Kerosuo, H., Kajamaa, A., & Engeström, Y. (2010). Promoting innovation and learning through change laboratory: An example from Finnish health care. *Central European Journal of Public Policy*, 4(1), pp. 110–131.

Kesting, P., & Ulhøi, J. (2010). Employee-driven innovation: Extending the license to foster innovation. *Management Decision*, 48, pp. 65–84. Doi: 10.1108/0025 1741011014463.

Kuhlman, S. (2010). Performance management in European local governments: A comparative analysis of reform experiences in Great Britain, France, Sweden and Germany. *International Review of Administrative Sciences*, 76(2), pp. 331–345. Doi: 10.1177/0020852310372050.

Lipsky, M. (2010). *Street-level bureaucracy: Dilemmas of the individual in public services. 30th Anniversary expanded edition*. New York: Russell Sage.

McGahey, R., & Willis, M. (2017). The promise and reality of social impact bonds. In V. Bartlett, A. Bugg-Levine, D. Erickson, I. Galloway, J. Genser, & J. Talansky, *What matters: Investing in results to build strong, vibrant communities* (pp. 420–427). San Francisco: Federal Reserve Bank of San Francisco and Nonprofit Finance Fund.

Moore, M. (2002). *Recognizing value in policing*. Washington, DC: Police Executive Research Forum.

NHS England Liaison and Diversion Programme. (2014). *Liaison and diversion operation model 2013/14*. London: The NHS Constitution. Retrieved from www. england.nhs.uk/wp-content/uploads/2014/04/ld-op-mod-1314.pdf

Osborne, D., & Gaebler, T. (1993). *Reinventing government*. Reading, MA: Addison Wesley.

Osborne, S. (2010). *The new public governance?* London: Routledge.

Ploettner, J., & Tresseras, E. (2016). An interview with Yrjö Engeström and Annalisa Sannino on activity theory. *Bellaterra Journal of Teaching & Learning Language & Literature*, 9(4), pp. 87–98. Doi: 10.5565/rev/jtl3.709.

Pollitt, C., & Bouckaert, G. (2000). *Public management reform: A comparative analysis*. Oxford: Oxford University Press. Doi: 10.1016/S0024-6301(00)00083-2.

Querol, M., Virkkunen, J., Vilela, R., & Lopes, M. (2014). O laboratório de mudança como ferramenta para transformação colaborativa de atividades de trabalho: uma entrevista com Jaakko Virkkunen. *Saúde E Sociedade*, 23(1), pp. 336–344. Doi: 10.1590/S0104-12902014000100027.

Rice, D. (2013). Street-level bureaucrats and the welfare state: Toward a micro-institutionalist theory of policy implementation. *Administration and Society*, 45(9), pp. 1–38. Doi: 10.1177/0095399712451895.

Rittel, H., & Webber, M. (1973). Dilemmas in a general theory of planning. *Policy Sciences*, 4, pp. 155–169. Doi: 10.1007/BF01405730.

Rocha, P. (2020). Where is the primary contradiction? Reflections on the intricacies of research predicated on activity theory: Outlines. *Critical Practice Studies*, 21(2), pp. 6–28.

Rocha, P., & Holmen, A. (2020). Performance-based policy in offender rehabilitation: Limitation or innovation for front-line workers in liaison and diversion services? *Probation Journal.* Doi: 10.1177/0264550520926578.

Sannino, A., Daniels, H., & Gutierrez, K. (2009). Activity theory between historical engagement and future-making practice. In A. Sannino, H. Daniels, & K. Gutierrez, *Learning and expanding with activity theory* (pp. 1–18). New York: Cambridge University Press. Doi: 10.1017/CBO9780511809989.002.

Schumpeter, J. (1934). *The theory of economic development: An inquiry into profits, capital, credit, interest, and the business cycle.* Cambridge, MA: Harvard University Press.

Styhre, A. (2009). Tinkering with material resources. *The Learning Organization,* 16(5), pp. 386–397. Doi: 10.1108/09696470910974171.

Sundbo, J. (1997). Management of innovation in services. *The Service Industry Journal,* 17(3), pp. 432–455. Doi: 10.1080/02642069700000028.

Sundbo, J., & Fuglsang, L. (2002). *Innovation as strategic reflexivity.* London: Routledge.

Thomas, J. C. (2012). *Citizen, customer, partner: Engaging the public in public management.* New York: M. E. Sharpe.

Toivonen, M., & Tuominen, T. (2009). Emergence of innovations in services. *The Service Industries Journal,* 29(7), pp. 887–902. Doi: 10.1080/02642060902749492.

Tolviainen, H. (2007). Interorganisational leaning across levels: An object orientated approach. *Journal of Workplace Learning,* 19(6), pp. 343–358. Doi: 10.1108/13665620710777093.

van de Ven, A., Polley, D., Garud, R., & Venkataraman, S. (2008). *The innovation journey.* Oxford: Oxford University Press. Doi: 10.2307/259214.

van Dooren, W., Bouckeart, G., & Halligan, J. (2010). *Performance management in the public sector.* London: Routledge. Doi: 10.4324/9781315817590.

Vygotsky, L. (1987). Thinking and speech. In R. Rieber, & A. Carton, *The collected works of L. S. Vygotsky, volume 1: Problems of general psychology* (pp. 39–285). New York: Plenun Press.

Walker, R. (2006). Innovation type and diffusion: An empirical analysis of local government. *Public Administration,* 84, pp. 311–335. Doi: 10.1111/j.1467-9299.2006.00004.x.

Wenger, E. (2000). Communities of practice and social learning systems. *Organization,* 7(2), pp. 225–246. Doi: 10.1177/135050840072002.

3 Empirical evidence
A detailed case study of a successful alternative to imprisonment

In this chapter, the research's paradigm, methodological choices, data collection procedures, code development processes and data analysis strategy are addressed. A case study approach to data collection (Yin, 2009) was adopted. Observations, document analysis and interviews were employed as data collection methods. Information was captured through audio recording and continuous note-taking. A template analysis (King, 2012) was employed to analyse the transcripts of the interviews, while the data collected through observation and note-taking enabled a more detailed and context-driven interpretation of the events discussed in the interviews.

The chapter also presents the main findings of the case study around which this book is centred, although the implications of such evidence are mostly discussed in the next chapters.

3.1 The research paradigm and design

A research paradigm consists of its ontological and epistemological stances. Ontologically, activity theory conceives the nature of reality through concepts of "artefact mediation" and "object-oriented activity" to demonstrate how human beings are both shaped by and shape the world, respectively (Engeström, 1987), which intertwines cultural activities and psychological phenomena (Vygotsky, 1987). The separation of individual and social should never happen (Daniels, 2001), and human behaviour needs to be contextualised within broader social and cultural contexts (Cole, 1996). Epistemologically, activity theory defends that learning is a social-cultural process that happens in the real world through collective activities conducted around a shared object, therefore promoting studies that are qualitative rather than quantitative in their nature (Denzin & Lincoln, 2005). As a social-cultural practice, learning requires contextualising the psychological processes of an individual within the broader social and cultural settings in which they take place. In doing so, the research yields accounting for the

DOI: 10.4324/9781003186793-3

whole context in development (Engeström, 1999). Consequently, activity theory provides concepts that are especially useful when carrying out cross-organisational comparison because they allow for a full picture instead of a compartmentalised one.

Having said that, it might seem contradictory to adopt activity theory (a systems-level theory) in a study emphasising the perspective of front-line professionals (individuals), but it is not. To understand the individual processes undergone by front-line professionals, a case-study approach was the design choice for the empirical research project reflected in this book, as it allowed for in-depth study of a specific case (Harrison & Easton, 2004), namely the interagency collaboration of criminal justice and welfare services through the perspective of front-line professionals from one organisation in specific, that is, liaison and diversion services.

As explained by Yin (2009), single-case studies are appropriate in five instances, as follows: 1) when there is a "critical case," meaning a case presenting a set of circumstances that are critical to the study's theoretical underpinning; 2) when there is an "extreme case," that is, a case especially attractive because deviates from theoretical norms or everyday occurrences; 3) when there is a "representative case," that is, a case that captures the circumstances and conditions of an everyday situation; 4) when there is a "revelatory case," meaning a case that reveals a phenomenon previously inaccessible to social science inquiry; and 5) when there is a "longitudinal case," that is, studying the same single case at two or more different points in time. This book builds upon the findings of a representative single-case study that captured the circumstances and conditions of the interactions between front-line workers from L&D and other services in criminal justice and welfare systems.

Achieving breadth and depth in a single case study is not linked to the number of respondents or a large sample size but it regards focus. It is generally believed that single-case studies produce findings that emphasise specific details within a unique context (Easton, 2010), but single-case studies can also yield a breadth when the analysis is broad and fundamental themes are explored through the perspective of an individual entity, for example, the analysis of interagency collaboration (a broader phenomenon) through the perspective of a particular entity (L&D). It is with this inclination that the findings discussed in this book need to be faced in order to be deemed transferable. The breadth and depth of the insights presented here might forego immediate empirical generalisation, as they retain the intricate texture of the context in focus, but their transferability is grounded in the representativeness of the L&D site chosen (a member of the "wave one" sites that were originally chosen to roll out the new L&D national model due to their excellence in service provision and representativeness) as well as the relatability of the challenges discussed herein, which are most likely faced by other agencies providing the same type of services.

3.2 Criminal justice liaison and diversion services: a case study

To select the appropriate L&D site to serve as the focus of a representative single-case study, two criteria were followed: 1) only L&D services that were part of the wave one sites rolling out the new L&D national model were considered, and 2) only L&D services with well-established local support mechanisms in connection with other services in criminal justice and welfare systems were adequate. Wave one sites were originally selected by the government to roll out the national model due to their excellence in service provision and representativeness (Disley et al., 2016); therefore, a reliable indicator of a single-case study that was representative of the L&D services needed to be selected.

Once a site was chosen, the relevant data were accrued from participants and documents. As to participants, they were divided into two groups: L&D front-line staff and front-line workers from other services in the criminal justice and welfare systems. To be considered a front-line worker, they had to comply with the following criteria: 1) being workers who interact directly with the public they serve and 2) providing technical support to service users rather than having their responsibilities limited to administrative tasks. As to documents, they were used to support the creation of a more in-depth understanding of the contextual and historical background of the implementation of the new model for L&D and how it has impacted the relationship between the L&D site and neighbouring agencies in criminal justice and welfare systems.

The L&D site focus of the case study was located in southwest England and was selected because it belonged the wave one of sites that have been able to successfully roll out the L&D national model over the past six years, although the service already existed before that. Its team consisted of four administration staff; eight support, time and recovery workers (professionals who support adults and young people with mental health problems and/ or a learning disability through offering practical support and advice in the community); eight mental health practitioners; two team leaders; and one service manager. Due to the small size of the staff, the team leaders and the service manager also functioned as mental health practitioners when necessary, which transformed them into front-line workers for the purposes of this book. The organisation covered a county of 1000 square miles, which encompassed urban and rural areas serviced by 15 police stations, and served a population of approximately 780,000. In 2017, the service assessed 2,365 adults, and numbers increase yearly (Williams et al., 2019).

From the selected L&D site, the participant criteria narrowed the number of front-line workers to 19. All of them agreed to participate in the study. From the other services in criminal justice and welfare systems, nine professionals agreed to participate in the research project, two from the criminal justice system and seven from welfare services. In total, this book discusses the perspective of 28 participants spread across various services in both the criminal justice and welfare systems. Out of the total participants, 11 were male and 17 female. Age ranged from 25 to 56 years. All of them were British, although a few had an immigrant background. The vast majority had a university degree in a health-related field, but five of them were at the secondary education level. Their work experience varied greatly, ranging from 1 year to 32 years of work experience (although not necessarily working at the same organisation).

Semi-structured interviews were conducted with the participants. Responses were prompted through an interactive process between the interviewer and the interviewees. A tailored interview guide was drafted before each interview based on the specific characteristics of the upcoming interviewee. Consequently, the guide changed slightly as insight broadened, making it possible to build upon the information acquired as the interviews went on. Despite minor alterations, all interviews were conducted based on a framework informed by activity theory. Above all, the informants were intentionally left with ample room to elaborate or bring up new insights (Smith & Elger, 2014).

As this study was concerned with the perspective of front-line professionals working at the interface between criminal justice and welfare systems, the accounts of managers, as well as service users, were purposefully left out.

As to selected documents, the list included internal documents as well as policy documents such as official white papers, audits and evaluations, all describing the process of implementation of the new model for L&D ($n = 27$) in the selected site. Moreover, statistical reports of the screening and assessments taking place in custody and court upon the national model ($n = 12$) were collected to provide a perspective of the progress of the service upon the implementation of the new national model.

Observations were also conducted, but there was no formal schedule being followed. The approach chosen for the observation exercise was an unstructured type. As explained by Gillham, the goal with unstructured observation is to record behaviour holistically without the use of pre-determined guidelines, but no research, however open ended, lacks structure (Benson, 2010). Thus, despite the unstructured approach, three main points were observed:

the relationships professionals would establish while performing their jobs, the perception front-line workers from other agencies would have of L&D and the drivers and barriers practitioners would encounter in their daily work routine. Nevertheless, although providing interesting insights into practice at the interface between the criminal justice and welfare systems, the observations served more as one means to ensure embeddedness in the context as well as a credibility check.

Data collection took place between 2017 and 2019. Table 3.1 provides an overview of the methodology.

The transcribed interviews were subjected to a template analysis, which is a way of thematically analysing qualitative data that involves the development of a coding "template" summarising themes identified by the researcher as important in a data set and organises them in a meaningful and useful manner (King, 2012). In the end, a framework consisting of two main templates was produced, one template for L&D services and another for "other services" (Rocha, 2020).

Table 3.1 Data collection procedure summary

Methodology	*Sources*	*Procedure*
Document analysis	Materials available at the investigated L&D site, which provided an overview of the transition period the service went through between being a locally managed organisation to being a wave-one site following the new L&D model. The dataset included internal documents describing the process of implementation of the L&D national model and statistical reports on the number of clients being screened and assessed in custody and court upon the rollout.	Documents were categorised and any descriptive statistics related to the impact the new L&D model had on the performance/work routine of the investigated site was collated to the dataset.
Semi-structured interviews	Front-line workers at both the criminal justice ($n = 2$) and welfare services ($n = 7$) and L&D ($n = 19$).	Tape-recorded and transcribed semi-structured interviews.
Observations	Observed participants' interactions with other services and the tools available to facilitate communication within and between agencies.	Notetaking. The notes were used to contextualise data obtained through document analysis and interview.

3.2.1 Handling personal bias and ensuring trustworthiness

A well-known feature of qualitative studies is that they accommodate the researcher's personal perspective, which makes it hard to separate the final product from the scholar. Therefore, it is relevant for the researcher to be transparent and reflexive about the processes through which data have been gathered, analysed and presented (Polit & Beck, 2014).

Bias, understood as an influence capable of distorting the result of a study (Polit & Beck, 2014), is a term originally belonging to the paradigm of quantitative research. In this vein, the recognition of personal bias in qualitative studies is somewhat under dispute, as it does not fit the philosophical underpinnings of qualitative inquiry (Thorne et al., 2015). Relevant, though, is the understanding that concepts such as rigour and trustworthiness are more pertinent to the reflexive, subjective nature of qualitative researcher (Galdas, 2017). Appropriate methodological choices are the way to establish the trustworthiness (which can be sub-divided into credibility, dependability, transferability and confirmability) of a research project (Guba, 1981; Shenton, 2004).

In the case of the study reported in this book, credibility was ensured by making sure that findings were congruent with the reality being scrutinised (Shenton, 2004). To that end, research methods were well established before data collection started; that is, clear sampling criteria were used for both informants and documents comprising the dataset, interviews followed a specific schedule and data analysis followed predetermined procedures. Moreover, whenever possible, more than one method of data collection (methodological triangulation) was adopted, more than one source of data (data triangulation) was used and more than one type of theory was applied to interpret the investigated phenomenon (theory triangulation) (Van Maanen, 1983; Denzin & Lincoln, 2005). Also, to ensure participants' voluntary and honest participation, they were given opportunities to refuse to be part of the research. They were also given a chance to withdraw at any point. In addition, participants' honesty was spurred by letting them know that data would be anonymised.

Credibility and dependability are closely related, and by demonstrating the former, the researcher is ensuring the latter (Lincoln & Guba, 1985). As to dependability specifically, the research design has been reported in detail elsewhere (see Rocha, 2020), which enables future researchers to replicate the research, even though it might not guarantee the same results (Shenton, 2004).

Transferability is a controversial topic in qualitative research. While some argue that it is not possible (Erlandson et al., 1993), others suggest that transferability should not be dismissed entirely in qualitative studies

(Stake, 1994; Denscombe, 1998). Despite the discussion, sufficient contextual information about the fieldwork site, about the phenomenon being studied and about the background factors impinging on the study was produced, all to allow comparison to be made (Shenton, 2004). Additionally, to enable transferability, enough information on the methods adopted has been provided herein and elsewhere (Rocha, 2020; Rocha & Holmen, 2020), which is demonstrated by the undertaking of issues such as:

• The number of participating organisations and their location.
• Any limitations of the study or conflict of interest.
• Selection criteria and information on the participants.
• Data collection methods, the period over which they happened and the length of the data collection sessions.

Finally, confirmability refers to the objectivity of the data. However, ensuring the objectivity of a study is difficult, as researcher biases are inevitable, especially in qualitative research (Patton, 2002). To reduce the effect of possible bias and ensure that the findings of the study resulted from the experiences and ideas of the informants, both methodological data and theory triangulations were carried out. Also, personal beliefs underpinning decisions made and methods adopted have been acknowledged and explained (Rocha, 2020).

3.3 Research results

This book is unique insofar as it uses activity theory to address the perspective of front-line workers on interagency collaboration across criminal justice and welfare systems. In order to investigate the role of liaison and diversion as a connector between services, two issues guided the empirical investigation: first, how members of the L&D services perceived their role as facilitators of interagency collaboration across the criminal justice and welfare systems in light of the standardised guidelines introduced by the new national model and second, what the main contradictions found by L&D front-line workers were when trying to collaborate with neighbouring services to improve health and social care outcomes. By addressing these issues, evidence was produced in the direction that collaboration is far from optimal, the reason being fragmentation between services and inadequate information sharing. Table 3.2 provides an overview of the findings and how they contribute to the literature on interagency collaboration across criminal justice and welfare services.

The research produced evidence of the inability of agencies to collaborate in order to address the criminogenic needs of those entering the criminal

Table 3.2 Summary of the findings and their contribution to the knowledge

Findings	Contribution
The L&D national model did not promote the expected change in the dynamics between services, mostly because it did not provide agencies with appropriate conditions to implement the rules of the policy. Joint communication systems are not in place, information sharing is subpar and integrated care is negatively affected by that.	The use of activity theory to map the contextual background and identify potential contradictions within and between both the L&D, criminal justice and welfare services activity systems that serve as potential triggers for future development. Three activity systems were identified to represent the historical development of L&D services over time. They depicted the scenario 1) before the rollout of the L&D national model, 2) during the rollout of the L&D national model and 3) after the rollout of the L&D national model.
Services do not have their roles clearly specified, which causes miscommunication between professionals working in different agencies. There is a mismatch between local circumstances and the rules of the national model, which hinders the implementation of the model by front-line workers	The use of activity theory to articulate the drivers and barriers to prearrest/ pre-sentence models of rehabilitation of offenders from the perspective of the work done by L&D.
There is a conflict between standardised top-down policies and practice at the street level. In the context of rehabilitation of offenders, workers often abide by values and ethical standards of their profession, which leads to employee-based innovation, since professionals develop coping strategies to equate policy and reality.	The use of activity theory to explore the impact of top-down performance-based policing in public services, giving voice to front-line workers.

justice system as well as their incapacity to implement rehabilitation strategies that tackle clusters of correlated needs through integrated care. This finding specifically feeds into the literature on how to meet criminogenic needs to reduce recidivism (Andrews & Bonta, 2014; Hare, 2002; Skeem & Peterson, 2012).

The way criminogenic needs relate to risk factors is that they are both tied together; therefore, in trying to identify the reasons leading up to an offence, criminologists analyse the necessities of the offender and determine the individual's unmet needs that led to criminal behaviour. Thus, criminogenic needs are the characteristics directly connected to the probability of a person to re-offend (Andrews & Bonta, 2014).

The current research project provided evidence that organisations use independent IT systems, despite computer systems being the default means of information gathering and sharing. This has curbed agencies' ability to coordinate care. Even within the same organisation, there is miscommunication when it comes to different areas, since computer systems have been largely developed in a piecemeal fashion with limited links between regions. As a consequence, there is misalignment within and between services, which leads to a partial understanding of each other's roles and responsibilities.

Top-down attempts to transform practice via policy have not taken into account the technological challenges existent in the current setup. Considering the complexity and the scale of services provided by organisations in criminal justice and welfare services, most of the investment in IT systems has been made on an individualised basis. In other words, discrete systems have been implemented across services without any form of central intervention. The fragmentation engendered by local arrangements over the years has turned computer systems into a collaboration impediment rather than an enabler. Alternatively, front-line workers have strived to establish interpersonal relationships in order to circumvent systemic limitations and promote collaboration between services but generally are not empowered by the systems and policies in place.

The issues with information sharing put organisations in a predicament as to each other's roles, responsibilities and level of influence. While on the one hand, welfare organisations assume the police's capacity to deal with vulnerable people, on the other hand, the police assume the same about welfare services. Such assumptions have led to individuals falling through the cracks of the service. As responsibilities seem to be up for grabs, the evidence produced indicates a need for more clarity about care pathways and the role of L&D in its goal of bridging criminal justice and welfare services.

Although the national government has worked over the years to standardise practice across sites, different locations still operate through old communication tools that vary from place to place, and tensions between services remain. This tension between new rules being implemented and the use of old tools of communication reverberates in the interactions between the activity systems of L&D and its neighbouring services in the criminal justice and welfare systems. Moreover, there seems to be a revival of new public management strategies in the setting of offender rehabilitation, which can be observed through a proclivity of policymakers to emphasise performance-based policing, despite its implementation challenges at the street level. The limitations imposed by a top-down approach that has been using competitive elements in the process of allocating public funds through policies are perhaps even more evident in the context studied, where workers often abide by values and ethical standards of their profession (Robinson et al., 2016), which naturally leads to employee-based innovation, since professionals develop coping strategies to equate policy and reality (Fuglsang & Sørensen, 2011; Gallouj & Weinstein, 1997; Lippke & Wegener, 2014; Lipsky, 2010; Styhre, 2009). In the end, professionals tend to differentiate between "core-work tasks and housekeeping chores" and prioritise the former to detriment of the latter. This can be understood as a coping strategy to equate policy and reality, since front-line workers tend to operate under bureaucratic constraints and with limited resources.

Using activity theory to explore the relationship between L&D and other services in criminal justice and welfare services is beneficial, as it provides tools to give voice to the front-line workers who have been struggling to share knowledge due to a misalignment between the tools used by each organisation. Activity theory prioritises knowledge sharing as a means to promote collaboration and the consequent co-creation of a shared object, which is an innovative way to address the challenges provoked by fragmented communication systems. In fact, the tensions created by the misaligned communication tools create opportunities for expansive learning, which calls for the innovation of current working routines as well as the creation of new sorts of tools that ultimately can take interagency collaboration into consideration.

3.4 Final considerations

In light of the over-arching aim of this book (i.e., to explore how interagency collaboration between L&D and neighbouring services is perceived by street-level L&D workers after the introduction of a new national model for liaison and diversion) and the inherent issues addressed while investigating the perspective of the L&D front-line workers (i.e., how they perceive themselves as facilitators of interagency collaboration across criminal justice and welfare systems and what contradictions they encountered while doing so), the book's main contribution is perhaps the suggestion of new solutions to old problems through activity theory.

In this sense, the book provides not only an empirical but also a theoretical contribution to the field – empirical because the book draws upon a research project that addressed various aspects of the collaboration between agencies in both the criminal justice and welfare systems and theoretical because, as shown in Table 3.2, the activity theoretical framework developed in this book is a fresh way to address recurrent problems in the context of offender rehabilitation. The aim of this chapter is, therefore, to provide the readers with detailed information on the methodological choices of the research to enable them to replicate the study in other settings.

The use of activity theory to make sense of interagency collaboration happening at the street level between organisations in both criminal justice and welfare systems is innovative inasmuch as few studies are using the theory in the context of offender rehabilitation (Hean et al., 2015; Hean et al., 2017). Moreover, the focus on the role of the L&D front-line workers as a conduit for collaboration between agencies provides a fresh take on a topic that otherwise has been explored with an emphasis on practice at the organisational level (Fenge et al., 2014; Kane et al., 2017).

In this vein, the knowledge produced herein meets the desire to find innovative ways to transform their interagency working practices, as service leaders have reiterated the need for change in organisational practices to address a lack of shared understanding on key concepts of confidentiality and referral (Bradley, 2009). They also felt they had failed to gain the perspectives of the front-line professionals, how these practices impacted offenders' experiences of interagency working and ways to probe the underlying reasons behind these challenges (Fenge et al., 2014; Hean et al., 2017; Kane et al., 2017). In the end, activity theory fosters a novel way to make sense of the current scenario and provides tools to transform practice.

3.5 References

Andrews, D., & Bonta, J. (2014). *The psychology of criminal conduct*. London: Routledge. Doi: 1 0.4324/9781315721279.

Benson, S. (2010). Observation techniques: Structured to unstructured by B. Gillham. *The Journal of Educational Research*, 103(1), pp. 63–64. Doi: 10.2307/40539751.

Bradley, K. (2009). *The Bradley report: Lord Bradley's review of people with mental health problems or learning disabilities in the criminal justice system* (Vol. 7). London: Department of Health.

Cole, M. (1996). *Cultural psychology*. Cambridge, MA: The Belknap Press of Harvard University Press.

Daniels, H. (2001). *Vygotsky and pedagogy*. London: Routledge. Doi: 10.4324/97813 15617602.

Denscombe, M. (1998). *The good research guide for small-scale social research projects*. Buckingham: Open University Press.

Denzin, N. K., & Lincoln, Y. S. (2005). *Handbook of qualitative research*. Thousand Oaks: Sage Publications.

Disley, E., Taylor, C., Kruithof, K., Winpenny, E., Liddle, M., Sutherland, A., . . . Francis, V. (2016). *Evaluation of the offender liaison and diversion trial schemes*. Cambridge: RAND.

Easton, G. (2010). Critical realism in case study research. *Industrial Marketing Management*, 39(1), pp. 118–128. Doi: 10.1016/j.indmarman.2008.06.004.

Engeström, Y. (1987). *Learning by expanding: An activity-theoretical approach to developmental research.* Helsinki: Orienta-Konsultit. Doi: 10.1017/CBO9781139814744.

Engeström, Y. (1999). Activity theory and individual and social transformation. In Y. Engeström, R. Miettinen, & R. Punamäki, *Perspectives on activity theory* (pp. 19–38). Cambridge: Cambridge University Press. Doi: 10.1017/CBO9780511812774.003.

Erlandson, D., David A Erlandson, Edward L Harris, Barbara L Skipper & Steve D Allen. (1993). *Doing naturalistic inquiry: A guide to methods.* London: Sage.

Fenge, L.-A., Hean, S., Staddon, S., Clapper, A., Heaslip, V., & Jack, E. (2014). Mental health and the criminal justice system: The role of interagency training to promote practitioner understanding of the diversion agenda. *Journal of Social Welfare and Family Law*, 36(1), pp. 36–46. Doi: 10.1080/09649069.2014.891338.

Fuglsang, L., & Sørensen, F. (2011). The balance between bricolage and innovation: Management dilemmas in sustainable public innovation. *Service Industries Journal*, 31(4), pp. 581–595. Doi: 10.1080/02642069.2010.504302.

Galdas, P. (2017). Revisiting bias in qualitative research: Reflections on its relationship with funding and impact. *International Journal of Qualitative Methods*, 16, pp. 1–2. Doi: 10.1177/1609406917748992.

Gallouj, F., & Weinstein, O. (1997). Innovation in services. *Research Policy*, 26, pp. 537–556. Doi: 10.1016/S0048-7333(97)00030-9.

Guba, E. (1981). Criteria for assessing the trustworthiness of naturalistic inquiries. *Educational Communication and Technology Journal*, 29, pp. 75–91. Doi: 10.1007/BF02766777.

Hare, R. (2002). Psychopathy and risk for recidivism and violence. In N. Gray, J. Laing, & L. Moaks, *Criminal justice, mental health and politics of risk* (pp. 27–47). London: Cavendish.

Harrison, D., & Easton, G. (2004). Temporally embedded case comparison in industrial marketing research. In S. Fleetwood, & S. Ackroyd, *Critical realist applications in organisation and management studies* (pp. 194–210). New York: Routledge.

Hean, S., Ødegård, A., & Willumsen, E. (2017). Improving collaboration between professionals supporting mentally ill offenders. *International Journal of Prisoner Health*, 13(2), pp. 91–104. Doi: 10.1108/IJPH-12-2016-0072.

Hean, S., Willumsen, E., Ødegård, A., & Bjørkly, S. (2015). Using social innovation as a theoretical framework to guide future thinking on facilitating collaboration between mental health and criminal justice services. *International Journal of Forensic Mental Health*, 14(4), pp. 280–289. Doi: 10.1080/14999013.2015.1115445.

Kane, E., Evans, E., & Shokraneh, F. (2017). Effectiveness of current policing-related mental health interventions: A systematic review. *Criminal Behaviour and Mental Health*, 28(2), pp. 108–119. Doi: 10.1002/cbm.2058.

King, N. (2012). Doing template analysis. In G. Symon, & C. Cassell, *Qualitative organizational research: Core methods and current challenges* (pp. 426–450). London: Sage Publications.

Lincoln, Y., & Guba, E. (1985). *Naturalistic inquiry.* Beverly Hills: Sage.

Lippke, L., & Wegener, C. (2014). Everyday innovation: Pushing boundaries while maintaining stability. *Journal of Workplace Learning*, 26(6–7), pp. 376–391. Doi: 10.1108/JWL-10-2013-0086.

Lipsky, M. (2010). *Street-level bureaucracy: Dilemmas of the individual in public services. 30th Anniversary expanded edition.* New York: Russell Sage.

Patton, M. (2002). *Qualitative research and evaluation methods.* Thousand Oaks, CA: Sage.

Polit, D., & Beck, C. (2014). *Essentials of nursing research: Appraising evidence for nursing practice.* Philadelphia, PA: Wolters Kluwer/Lippincott/Williams & Wilkins Health.

Robinson, G., Burke, L., & Millings, M. (2016). Criminal justice identities in transition: The case of devolved probation services in England and Wales. *British Journal of Criminology*, 56(1), pp. 161–178. Doi: 10.1093/bjc/azv036.

Rocha, P. (2020). Exploring collaboration within and between criminal justice and welfare systems: The perspective of front-line liaison and diversion workers (Doctoral thesis, University of Stavanger, Norway), ISBN 978-82-7644-960-0.

Rocha, P., & Holmen, A. (2020). Performance-based policy in offender rehabilitation: Limitation or innovation for front-line workers in liaison and diversion services? *Probation Journal.* Doi: 10.1177/0264550520926578.

Shenton, A. (2004). Strategies for ensuring trustworthiness in qualitative research projects. *Education for Information*, 22, pp. 63–75. Doi: 10.3233/EFI-2004-22201.

Skeem, J. L., & Peterson, J. K. (2012). Identifying, treating, and reducing risk for offenders with mental illness. In J. Petersilia, & K. Reitz, *The Oxford handbook of sentencing and corrections.* Oxford: Oxford Handbooks Online. Doi: 10.1093/oxfordhb/9780199730148.013.0021.

Smith, C., & Elger, T. (2014). Critical realism and interviewing subjects. In K. Edwards, J. Mahoney, & S. Vincent, *Studying organizations using critical realism: A practical guide* (pp. 109–131). Oxford: University Press. Doi: 10.1093/acp rof:oso/9780199665525.003.0006.

Stake, R. (1994). Case studies. In N. Denzin, & Y. Lincoln, *Handbook of qualitative research* (pp. 236–247). Thousand Oaks: Sage.

Styhre, A. (2009). Tinkering with material resources. *The Learning Organization*, 16(5), pp. 386–397. Doi: 10.1108/09696470910974171.

Thorne, S., Stephens, J., & Truant, T. (2015). Building qualitative study design using nursing's disciplinary epistemology. *Journal of Advanced Nursing*, 72(2), pp. 451–460. Doi: 10.1111/jan.12822.

Van Maanen, J. (1983). The fact and fiction in organizational ethnography. In J. Van Maanen, *Qualitative methodology* (pp. 37–55). Beverly Hills: Sage. Doi: 10.4324/9781315241371-24.

Vygotsky, L. (1987). Thinking and speech. In R. Rieber, & A. Carton, *The collected works of L. S. Vygotsky, volume 1: Problems of general psychology* (pp. 39–285). New York: Plenun Press.

Williams, N., Sadler, S., Durcan, G., & Mayers, A. (2019). Health and justice characteristics of Dorset's liaison and diversion population. Unpublished manuscript.

Yin, R. (2009). *Case study research and applications: Design and methods.* London: Sage Publications.

4 Moving the state of the art forward

Suggestions on co-created alternatives to imprisonment as a means to rehabilitate offenders in the community

The idea of having the criminal justice and welfare services working together to address the needs of vulnerable people entering the justice system is well accepted among policymakers (Ministry of Justice UK, 2013; NHS England Liaison and Diversion Programme, 2014) as well as scholars (Hean et al., 2009; Rocha & Holmen, 2020; Strype et al., 2014). In practice, the notion has been, by and large, manifested through policymakers' proclivity to implement strategies aimed at promoting collaboration between agencies. As explained in this book, however, governments expect that these top-down injunctions will naturally gain force at the street level of public service organisations, but there seems to be a gap between policy instructions and their actual implementation in practice (Hill & Huppe, 2014). This fact can be usually justified on the basis of the work conditions faced by front-line workers, as they tend to operate under bureaucratic constraints and with limited resources (Lipsky, 2010).

Such challenges could be observed in practice by the author of this book, who investigated the obstacles to collaboration faced by front-line workers across the criminal justice and welfare systems in England. The case of liaison and diversion services and their recently introduced operation model epitomises the scenario described in the previous paragraph: that the top-down implementation of policies will remain unsuccessful at the street level as long as it does not account for local circumstances and front-line workers' discretion.

This book suggests that the deviance from policy intent at the street level has been construed as a form of innovation instead of implementation failure (Hupe & Hill, 2016). This is a notion that builds upon the traditional understanding of front-line workers as lower-level policymakers (Lipsky, 2010) and, as proposed herein, is a judicious way to move the state of the art forward. In this context, the use of activity theory to make sense of it, especially in the offender rehabilitation setting, is not only innovative but also commensurate. Thus, interpreting professionals' coping strategies as

DOI: 10.4324/9781003186793-4

value-driven work practices aimed at handling managerial instructions that are misaligned with reality is a way of making sense of the incremental transformation that begins as an adjustment of the policy to the workers' reality and develops into autonomous practices and routines (Fuglsang, 2010).

Dealing with specific top-down implementation instructions in their overloaded work situation, the L&D front-line staff used their discretionary judgment based on professional values and ethics to decide whether specific instructions of the national model for L&D were feasible. There was a prioritisation of tasks engrossed in their goal of supporting vulnerable people (the "core-work tasks"), while ancillary tasks ("housekeeping chores") tended to be kept at bay (Rocha & Holmen, 2020). The prioritisation was carried out by professionals themselves and overtly reported throughout the research project in which this book is grounded (see Chapter 3 for more details). In certain ways, it is bewildering to fathom that the enforcement of an entire system can be contingent on the ethics of the workers, which comes to reinforce the relevance of this book.

In this chapter, the background information, the theoretical discussions and the empirical evidence introduced in the previous chapters are brought together. The use of activity theory to perform such a task is a germane choice, since the theory provides the readers with appropriate tools to not only understand the current scenario but also to envision the transformed practice that lurks in the future.

4.1 The impact of top-down policies on street-level interagency collaboration through the lenses of activity theory

The idea of everyday employee-based innovation at the front line emerging from casuistic problem-solving can also be perceived as an incremental type of innovation that draws upon the resolution of present contradictions, which is in line with activity theory (Engeström, 1999; Ellström, 2010). Now, let us use the liaison and diversion services case to exemplify that.

First of all, there is tension within the L&D activity system. This contradiction has been manifested as a mismatch between the national model for L&D (rule) and the service's goal to liaise with other agencies to divert vulnerable people into care (object), as graphically represented in Figure 4.1. It is through the resolution of the current contradictions in the L&D activity system that a new and evolved system can be developed. In this new scenario, the national model can finally be appropriately incorporated by front-line professionals thanks to the resolution of the existent challenges.

In the current setup, there is a state of need lurking at the bottom of the L&D activity system. In other words, there is a contradiction within the

Tools
Computer systems, phone calls,
face-to-face interactions

Subject
Mental health practitioners and
support, time and
recovery workers

Object
Liaison with other services
on behalf of clients and
diversion of vulnerable clients
into care (when appropriate)

Rules
Bradley Report, Liaison &
Diversion Operation Model and
Standard Service Specification

Community
Custody staff, court staff,
referred-to agencies staff

Division of Labor
Interagency work,
peer support

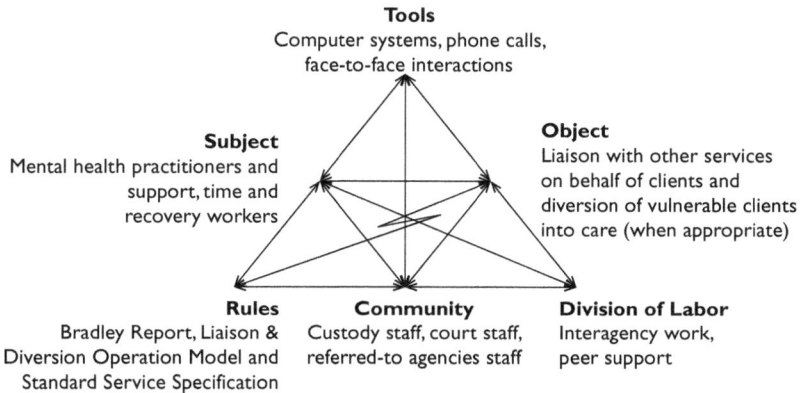

Figure 4.1 L&D activity system with a contradiction between rules and object
Source: (Adapted from Engeström, 1987).

L&D activity system and also between the L&D and the neighbouring services systems. In the need state, there is a questioning happening within a
constituent component of the L&D activity system, namely the professionals (subject). This form of questioning/tension has been defined as a primary contradiction (Engeström, 1987), which has the ability to kick off an
expansive learning cycle to transform the current L&D activity system. The
notion of primary contradiction and its empirical implications are of crucial
importance for activity theoretical studies but are beyond the scope of this
book; therefore, they have been discussed elsewhere (Rocha, 2020). However, in a nutshell, expansive learning cycles refer to the processes whereby
an activity system resolves its internal contradictions by constructing and
implementing a new way to function (Engeström, 1987), and they are generally kicked off by grappling with an identified primary contradiction.

In this book, the notion of primary contradiction is predicated upon the
antithetical relations between exchange-value and use-value in capitalist
socioeconomic formations (Engeström, 1987). The L&D front-line workers
have a use-value (a fundamental existence) that is currently opposing their
exchange value (their perception as commodities in a marketplace). In practical terms, L&D professionals work to support vulnerable clients (core-
work tasks) but are required to demonstrate positive outcomes in order for
the service to continue being funded (housekeeping chores). This contradiction between their core-work tasks (their use-value) and their housekeeping
chores (their exchange-value) makes professionals question their own role

in L&D the activity system. Are they working to support clients or to gather data that demonstrate positive outcomes and guarantee remuneration?

This need state (the existence of a primary contradiction) leads to a second phase where the primary contradiction transcends the limits of the constituent component and becomes a tension between elements of the system (a secondary contradiction). In the L&D activity system, this second stage is represented by the tension between professionals (subject) and the national model (rule).

The goal in this second stage is to analyse the reasons for the discrepancy between the instructions of the national model and the circumstances found at the street level, which enables the modelling of a solution. To that end, the findings of this study (see the previous chapter) provide data on the front-line workers' perspective as to why implementation at the street level is troublesome. Based on the data, those involved in the development and implementation of the model (L&D front-line workers, middle-level managers and policymakers) could collaborate to have a breakthrough where they model new solutions for the activity. In this case, new solutions could include, for example, the modelling of new instruments/strategies (tools) that enable the implementation of the national model or a different division of labour that allows front-line workers to focus only on core-work tasks.

In any event, the new solution modelled has to be examined and tested to ensure effectiveness. It is only after the necessary adjustments are made that a new model emerges. Then, this new model has to be implemented in the old (current) L&D activity system.

It is natural that during the implementation contradictions will occur between the old and the new models. These are called tertiary contradictions by Engeström (1987). An example of those could be L&D front-line workers resisting the use of novel instruments/strategies or being dissatisfied with the new proposed division of labour.

These tertiary contradictions lead to a stage of reflection on the impact the expansive learning cycle has had on the L&D activity system. Moreover, there is a need to consider the impact the cycle might have had on neighbouring organisations as well. Potential contradictions between the new L&D activity system and the activity systems of other organisations in criminal justice and welfare services are called quaternary contradictions (Engeström, 1987). It is by meditating the impact of the cycle on neighbouring activity systems that these quaternary contradictions can be tackled and the entire expansive learning cycle stabilised. Then, the result would be the consolidation of a new practice. The whole cycle is graphically represented by Figure 4.2.

7. CONSOLIDATING THE NEW L&D MODEL

PRIMARY CONTRADICTION – NEED STATE
1. QUESTIONING
    Are L&D schemes a way to support vulnerable people entering the criminal justice system or a commodity paid for by local governments through funding arrangements?

SECONDARY CONTRADICTION – DOUBLE BIND
2A. HISTORICAL ANALYSIS – *The nature of local systems and structures contradicts the idea of a unified service*
2B. EMPIRICAL ANALYSIS – *Local rules limit L&D schemes' ability to collaborate*

3. MODELLING THE NEW SOLUTION
    Development of a national model for L&D services that standardises practice across schemes and facilitates collaboration

QUATERNARY CONTRADICTION – REALIGNMENT WITH NEIGHBOURS
6. REFLECTING ON THE PROCESS

CRIMINAL JUSTICE

NEW L&D ACTIVITY SYSTEM

WELFARE SERVICES

TERTIARY CONTRADICTION–RESISTANCE
5. IMPLEMENTING THE NEW MODEL

PAST L&D ACTIVITY SYSTEM

NEW L&D ACTIVITY SYSTEM

4. EXAMINING THE NEW MODEL
    The rollout of the national model in ten trial sites

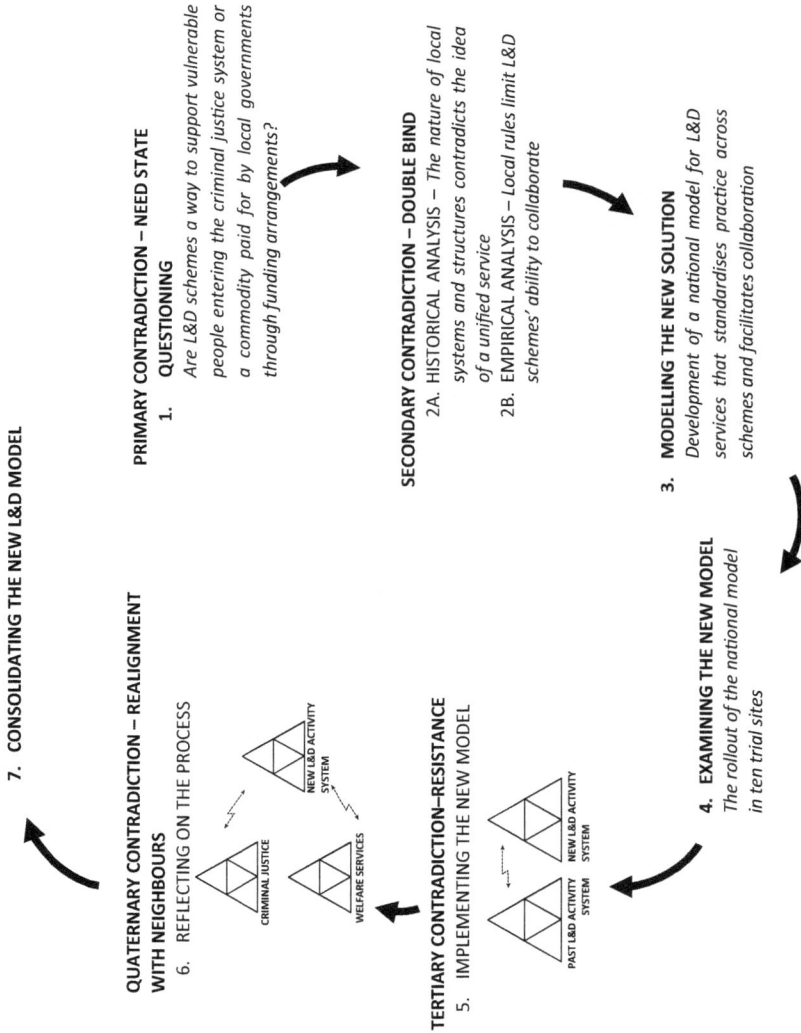

Figure 4.2 L&D potential expansive learning cycle
Source: (Adapted from Engeström, 2001).

Expansive learning cycles are developed through a dialogue between all the interested parties. In this vein, the previous representation of the L&D expansive learning cycle is not to be taken as a formula to be bestowed upon the organisation but solely as an example of how things could potentially unfold. It more of an intellectual exercise to demonstrate the rationale behind an activity theory-oriented intervention. Currently, however, front-line professionals in different L&D sites carry out an ad hoc implementation of the national model, as discussed in the previous chapter. Localised decision-making is constrained by the contingencies of each region, and practice among L&D sites is still disparate. The volatility of the current scenario – which the national model did not manage to extinguish – is the testimony to the benefit of innovation models that regard all the interested actors and are not imposed top down. That is an issue addressed in more detail in Section 4.4, where recommendations are made based upon the data emerging from this study.

4.2 What are the main contradictions encountered by front-line workers and how to address them?

This section addresses the challenges front-line professionals encounter in their work routine while collaborating to improve health and social care outcomes for service users. The results of the study provided evidence of three main contradictions hindering integrated care at the street level, namely 1) tensions between standard top-down policies and local circumstances found at the street level, 2) stretched workers due to high caseloads and 3) restrictions on information sharing due to confidentiality concerns and fragmentation of communication tools, which seems to be backed up by the scientific literature (Fuglsang, 2010; Lipsky, 2010; Thunman, 2013).

4.2.1 Top-down policies versus street-level circumstances: an obstacle to interagency collaboration

In the previous section, the focus was on the contradiction between the elements of the L&D activity system, namely L&D front-line workers (subject) striving to fit the instructions (rules) of the national model into their local circumstances in order for collaboration (object) to happen in accordance with the new policy. It was also suggested that the current L&D activity system could be transformed through expansive learning cycles and that the resolution of the tension between workers would give rise to an evolved L&D activity system. In such a scenario, quaternary contradictions would most likely occur, that is, tensions between the new L&D activity system and the activity systems of neighbouring agencies in criminal justice and welfare services.

In reality, however, an L&D activity system that includes a national model is already a novelty when compared to an L&D activity system where the service is locally organised. Thus, it is possible to affirm that there has been a quaternary contradiction between the current L&D activity system (including a national model) and activity systems of neighbouring agencies in criminal justice ever since the introduction of the new national model. The lack of clarity as to L&D's role and power since the national model has promoted its fair share of challenges for those collaborating with the service.

In the study, the data demonstrated that professionals from other organisations in criminal justice and welfare systems see the need for a defined care plan co-designed by the agencies operating in the context. They understand that such coordination could be facilitated by L&D bringing services together. However, the evidence produced demonstrated that the national model has actually instilled a conflict (a primary contradiction) into L&D professionals' minds, and they currently struggle between the liaison with other services to support clients (core-work task) and the gathering of data that demonstrate positive outcomes and guarantee remuneration of the service (housekeeping chore).

As they have to choose between core-work tasks and housekeeping chores, the L&D front-line workers seem stretched, and that leads to a contradiction between L&D's and other agencies' activity systems. In the midst of this, policy implementation at the street level has been subpar. There is a need to adapt the national model to local circumstances, which means not always following the policy. This has been hindering the possibility of other services making sense of L&D's role and ultimately impairing interagency collaboration.

An alternative view would be that, considering the steps of an expansive learning cycle described previously, the current quaternary contradiction between the L&D, criminal justice and welfare services activity systems exist because the national model (a new modelled solution – step 3) was not adequately examined (step 4) and/or did not suffer enough resistance within the L&D activity system (step 5). In this scenario, it would be necessary to investigate why L&D sites rolling out the national model did not resist the model. It is possible to speculate that the lack of internal resistance would be because the L&D sites did not have the political strength to go against the ideas of the main sponsor of the service, namely the national government. However, this is a conjecture that is not necessarily supported by the findings of this study.

4.2.2 The impact of high caseloads on policy implementation and interagency collaboration

Front-line workers' high caseload is a particular challenge mentioned in the literature (Lipsky, 2010) that was confirmed by this study. In the face of a constant backlog of cases to be dealt with, time for collaboration with professionals from other agencies becomes a commodity workers might not be able to afford (Hornby & Atkins, 2000). On top of that, in the context of rehabilitation of offenders, agencies are running IT systems that are not interconnected; that is, each organisation has its own independent database system. The result is a scenario in which information sharing is difficult, collaboration limited and integrated care hard to realise.

High caseloads also bear a consequence in policy implementation (Fuglsang, 2010). At the street level, front-line workers operate under bureaucratic constraints, with limited resources and the expectation of high productivity (Lipsky, 2010). In such conditions, front-line workers are inclined to deviate from top-down policies that do not necessarily match their or the clients' needs (Rocha & Holmen, 2020; Thunman, 2013). The deviation, which is, by and large, motivated by resource constraints, tends to make implementation subpar (Lippke & Wegener, 2014). The findings of this study aligned with the literature, especially in cases where front-line workers were stretched and had to prioritise between performing core-work tasks and integrally implementing the L&D national model. They serve to ratify the understanding that collaboration between public-sector organisations requires the alignment of politicians, management and employees (Hean et al., 2015), which could be facilitated by activity theory principles and tools (Engeström, 2001), as demonstrated in this book. Processes initiated top down without consideration for the circumstances existent at the street level will ultimately not be carried out as planned. They tend to overwhelm front-line workers and provoke a feeling of inauthenticity within the staff (Thunman, 2013). In this sense, seminal to the idea of interagency collaboration in public-sector organisations is the understanding and cooperation between top-down and bottom-up processes (Høyrup, 2010).

In summary, prearrest/pre-sentence strategies of rehabilitation require L&D, the police, courts and organisations in the welfare system to work in tandem to timely divert vulnerable individuals into appropriate care. However, the evidence suggests that the use of IT networks to communicate and exchange information is far from optimal, since multiple non-connected computer systems across services have caused misalignments and curbed collaboration.

4.2.3 Fragmented communication tools hampering information sharing

In the context of offender rehabilitation, co-designed care plans are crucial (Hean et al., 2009; Strype et al., 2014). However, in such a complex environment, determining what elements are influencing successful collaborative initiatives can be challenging.

Interagency collaboration, which entails coordination through several strata and across multiple organisations, is contingent on specific factors enabling successful interactions, for example, teamwork, tools supporting the work, the development of non-hierarchical relationships and knowledge sharing (Warburton et al., 2008). However, more often than not, barriers to collaboration impair organisations working in tandem.

As mentioned previously in this chapter, a few of these barriers impeding interagency collaboration are stretched workers due to high caseloads, restrictions on information sharing due to confidentiality concerns and high rates of staff turnover. Above all, the evidence suggests that the currently available tools of communication are not supporting collaboration within and between organisations. Although IT systems are the default means of communication within and between organisations, they are not interconnected. The benefits of having properly maintained clinical information systems supporting collaboration are undeniable (Woltmann et al., 2012), but the fragmentation between the diverse IT systems curbs information sharing and ultimately impairs collaboration.

In the offender rehabilitation setting, investment in modernisation programs over the years has been made on an individualised basis, and IT solutions have grown in a piecemeal fashion, with limited links between them. Keen explains that these systems were developed independently for logistic reasons, relating to the scale and complexity of implementation of a unified healthcare system across the country. Consequently, discrete sectoral systems have been developed for GPs, outpatient clinics and other services so that they would not have to wait for national initiatives (2010). In this sense, the current fragmentation can be understood as a historical impediment to collaboration and requires adaptation to current needs.

In a scenario where technological limitations are prone to hampering co-designed care plans predicated on shared information versus, front-line workers have been looking for alternative ways to collaborate and exchange data. The use of phone calls as a means for professionals to interact with each other in a less rigid way and consequently obtain information on clients can be salutary. However, in the context of this study particularly, professionals' divergent work hours and availability tend to hinder communication through telephone. As noted by Fredheim et al. (2011), simply making a phone call to a staff member in another service can be challenging, even though phone calls are the glue of interagency collaboration.

In light of such challenges, front-line workers in criminal and welfare services have been striving to realise interagency collaboration through interpersonal relationships. To name a few of the observed behaviours they adopt to foster collaboration, for example, the front-line staff makes an intentional effort to expand their relationships with professionals from agencies beyond work-related matters and establish an informal way of communicating, which has allowed them to discuss formal, professional issues openly (yet effectively). Another example would be co-location, since professionals discussing face to face how to treat patients and co-create intervention strategies would contribute to building a sense of unity among themselves, even though they belong to different organisations. A third strategy deployed specifically by the L&D front-line staff would be performing small favours to professionals from other organisations from time to time, which puts the L&D staff in a position of having their needs met by other services trying to reciprocate the received favours (Cialdini, 2016).

However, it seems to be easier to achieve collaboration at the strategic level than it is at the street level, mostly because of the increased number of variables that have to align in order for collaboration to take place among front-line workers (Lipsky, 2010). In this sense, when considering collaboration, it is crucial to find solutions to drive information flow among those involved in the care of service users (Statham, 2011). The use of IT systems supporting client management is part of the answer but not in the current setup where each organisation runs a different computer program, and there is no communication between them. For new solutions to come up, it is pivotal, therefore, to include the perspective of those who are directly involved in the service delivery, namely front-line workers. Bottom-up solutions will address the problem found at the front line and ultimately yield effective alternatives to interagency collaboration (Ellström, 2010).

4.3 Practical and theoretical implications

Current rehabilitative strategies such as care pathways and care plans are top-down attempts to standardise collaboration at the street level (Hill & Huppe, 2014) that generate a negative reactive response from front-line workers. The point that this book is trying to drive is that a practice-based approach to innovation would pay tribute to these professionals' ethics and allow them to be more proactive (Lipsky, 2010). In other words, the involvement of front-line professionals in the development of innovative solutions to the rehabilitation of vulnerable people is crucial if they are to be implemented properly (Robinson et al., 2016).

The empirical findings discussed herein – 1) fragmentation of communication tools hampering information sharing within and between agencies, 2) policy implementation is difficult at the street level and leads to a certain degree of adaptation of top-down instruction to street-level contingencies and 3) front-line workers relying on interpersonal relationships to circumvent systemic limitations and promote collaboration between agencies – confirm the knowledge produced by the existent literature (Gallouj & Weinstein, 1997; Styhre, 2009; Lipsky, 2010; Fuglsang & Sørensen, 2011; Lippke & Wegener, 2014; Robinson et al., 2016) in addition to offering an up-to-date read on the situation in the criminal justice and welfare system settings, demonstrating that these challenges are still to be overcome.

A common thread interlinking the mentioned findings presented in this book is the need for the involvement of front-line professionals in the innovation process and the benefits of using activity theory to enable that. The integration must happen both within and between agencies in criminal justice and welfare systems (Hean et al., 2009; Hean et al., 2017). Collaboration within agencies can enable communication between management and operational levels and leads to the co-design of new solutions (Strype et al., 2014), and collaboration between agencies can bring organisations together and enable knowledge sharing (Warmington et al., 2004).

Although this overall message has been unpicked elsewhere (Rocha, 2020a; Rocha & Holmen, 2020), simply put, the mere introduction of a new top-down policy is not a guarantee of change at the street level, as it is possible to see in the case of the L&D services in England, where front-line workers are adapting the new national model for the service before putting it into practice. The involvement of street-level agents in the innovation and implementation processes is the key to success.

The suggestion of activity theory and its tools as a means to enable collaboration and address the communication challenges existent in the current setup is due to the theory's emphasis on dialectics and the flattening of power relations (Engeström, 1987), which empowers actors at the street level to take part in the process of innovation and provides them with the necessary tools to do so (Engeström, 2001).

In the next section, the specifics of how activity theory can help to tackle issues of fragmentation between IT systems and policy implementation in addition to fostering bottom-up transformation in the work practice of agencies in both criminal justice and welfare systems are further explored. Nevertheless, believing activity theory is flawless would also be naïve. Therefore, this book also has the responsibility to present alternatives to the advancement of the theory.

As Pinker pointed out (1995), the study of human nature in Western culture in the twentieth century was impregnated with what the author called the

"Standard Social Science Model," which posits that human behaviour is largely determined by culture-bound social learning. This is an understanding that dovetails nicely with the need for the theoretical advancement of activity theory.

There is no doubt human behaviour is largely influenced by external factors, but activity theorists seem to have overestimated the extent to which exogenous elements are influential (Bakhurst, 2009; Jones, 2009, 2011). They seem to have overlooked cross-cultural similarities that indicate the existence of higher order factors (most likely evolutionary-based biological tendencies) that transcend cultural-historical contexts (Costa & McCrae, 1992) or perhaps just relied too much on Vygotsky's work developed back in the nineteenth century.

The goal to use activity theory in the context of offender rehabilitation was to validate it in a new context. The theory must be responsive and relevant for new emerging phenomena, which can only be achieved through the development of new concepts and their trial in new settings. It was due to its use in a new context that this study was able to identify its potential shortfalls (Rocha, 2020b).

As a theory concerned with societal activities (Engeström, 2001; Engeström & Sannino, 2010), activity theory inherently struggles with limited exploration of subjectivity, which has already been acknowledged in the literature but not yet fully explored (Bakhurst, 2009; Jones, 2009, 2011; Roth, 2007). The traditional triangular representation of activity overlooks the issue of subjectivity, but it is to be acknowledged that such a characteristic is in line with the theory's philosophical grounding. Activity theory is fundamentally a Marxist theory that – in line with Marx's ideology – emphasises collective identity to the detriment of individual identity. Besides a few scholars (see, e.g., Allen et al., 2013; Bakhurst, 2009; Roth, 2007), criticism of activity theory's focus on societal matters at the expense of individuality is rather reticent, perhaps due to the postmodern ideology reigning within social sciences currently (Hicks, 2019), which also favours collective identity to the detriment of individual identity.

Accounting for the subjects' motivation to collaborate rather than just focusing on cultural, historical and contextual circumstances impeding or promoting collaboration between organisations is crucial, as motivation is a predominant factor in influencing individuals' behaviour towards their objectives. A holistic understanding of the subject's motivation in an activity has to necessarily run through the acknowledgement of biologically based psychological tendencies determining his/her behaviour.

4.4 Recommendations

In the public sector, innovation is traditionally initiated by central levels of the government in a top-down manner, such as the L&D national model discussed in this book. This approach presupposes standard instructions being equally applied across diverse contexts (Lipsky, 2010). However, the idea of having a one-size-fits-all model to be applied to local settings has already been contested elsewhere (Rittel & Webber, 1973), as the effectiveness of any solution is dependent on the environment and actors involved.

Although the findings explored herein pertain immediately to the case of L&D services, they seem to represent a sub-species of a broader genre already addressed in the literature, namely the need for collaboration between interested actors in the pursuit of innovation in the public sector (Ellström, 2010; Fuglsang, 2010; Hill & Huppe, 2014; Høyrup, 2010; Lipsky, 2010). The procedures carried out by the several L&D sites across England are the reflection of their local contexts and are deeply embedded in their work routines. Therefore, any attempt to innovate needs first to take into account the cultural and historical circumstances of each L&D site and only then break away from previous practices. One-size-fits-all models will most likely fail because they do not consider the local settings and the actors involved (Rittel & Webber, 1973), as supported by the findings of this research in the case of L&D services.

The L&D national model's endeavour to standardise practice nationwide fails because each site has different needs and conditions, according to the evidence produced by this study. The implications of such findings illustrate an imminent need for collaboration and innovation to be addressed as a bottom-up matter. Thus, it is salutary that decision-makers in public policy support employee-driven innovation processes and create an appropriate environment where open dialogue between actors at different strata is feasible. To that end, further research could support the attainment of such a scenario by exploring alternatives that do not rely on top-down initiatives but instead emphasise the resourcefulness of front-line professionals initiating solutions. On that note, this book suggests the change laboratory model as a suitable strategy to tackle the challenge of innovatively promoting integrated care in a fragmented setting (Kerosuo & Engeström, 2003; Tolviainen, 2007).

As a tool for promoting innovation and learning within and between organisations, the CLM draws upon activity-theoretical concepts and has been successfully applied in other interagency workplaces (Kerosuo & Engeström, 2003; Tolviainen, 2007; Virkkunen et al. 2014) by emphasising the benefits of solutions co-devised by all those involved in the implementation process, meaning politicians, managers, front-line workers and service users.

In its basic setup, the CLM provides participants with three sets of wallboards to represent their work activity. The horizontal dimensions of the wallboards depict different levels of abstraction and generalisation, whereas the vertical dimensions represent the change in time (past, present and future). In the mirror wallboard, participants find registers of their daily work practices, for example, videotaped episodes of work, interviews and stories. In the model/vision wallboard, activity-theoretical concepts are used to analyse the data from the mirror wallboard. Finally, in the ideas/ tools wallboard, participants find the resources created during the sessions, that is, intermediate cognitive tools such as schedules, schemes and charts (Engeström & Escalante, 1996). Figure 4.3 illustrates the CLM basic setting.

The CLM starts with participants analysing current contradictions in an activity. The goal is to find the roots of the problem, which is usually achieved by modelling previous iterations of the activity. Following up, the current activity is also modelled, and any existent contradictions are included. Then, participants envision the future model and develop a plan to achieve it. The entire process takes several sessions and lasts from three to six months (Engeström & Escalante, 1996). As a result, new solutions are created by expanding objects; developing new tools, rules or communities;

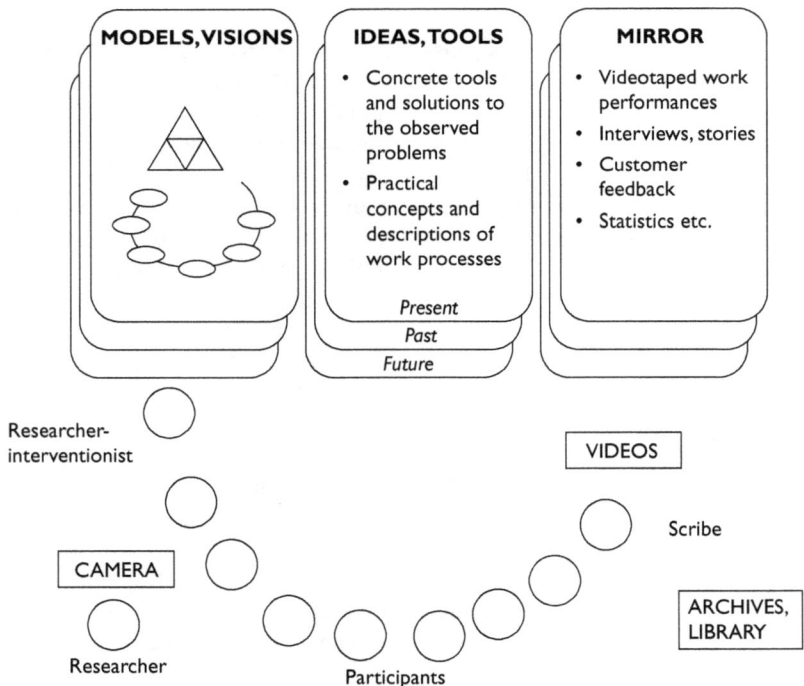

Figure 4.3 Basic setup for CLM

Source: (Adapted from Engeström & Escalante, 1996, p. 11).

or even by redesigning the division of labour (Engeström et al., 2007). Thus, CLM can be understood as a means to innovate, and this is how it could be done in the case of L&D, for example.

The findings produced by this research have the potential to inform the mirror wallboard. The historical documents gathered throughout this study form a commensurate dataset to inform the mirror wallboard in its past dimension, and the accounts produced by interviewees would dovetail nicely with the mirror wallboard in its present dimension. The future dimension of the mirror wallboard could comprise, for example, my analysis of the collected data, which is basically a discussion of the current shortfalls and conjectures of potential ways forward.

In the model/vision wallboard would go an activity-theoretical analysis – activity systems – of intra- and interagency collaboration in its current format, which would be facilitated by me and carried out by the CLM participants (front-line workers in the L&D and neighbouring criminal justice and welfare services, middle and top-level managers and policymakers). An idea of how these activity systems could look in terms of their vertical dimensions (past, present and future) is found elsewhere (Rocha, 2020a), which traces the historical development of L&D services through the lenses of CHAT.

Finally, in the ideas/tools wallboard, the results of the CLM sessions would be found. These would be intermediate tools to be put into practice. Their goal is to kick off the development of learning cycles that tackle existent contradictions and transform the current practice and, in the case of L&D, have the objective to foster more adequate policymaking and collaboration with other services.

The CLM is a highly iterative strategy based on activity theory tenets. Therefore, most of its stages are to be realised in tandem with participants and not pre-arranged by the researcher. In fact, the role of the researcher in a CLM intervention is solely to facilitate the participants' sense-making of their current work activity and development of solutions to address contradictions existent in the current setup. In the L&D case study, the tensions pointed out by the findings produced by this research are a crucial initial step in learning circles of transformation, thus the relevance of the contribution yielded herein.

It is important to acknowledge, however, that asymmetric power relations inhibit the creation of a multi-voiced environment where dialogue between powerless and powerful actors exists (Courpasson & Clegg, 2012). Thus, the existence of an open dialogue between all of those involved in the rehabilitation of offenders is a prerequisite to the deployment of an intervention such as CLM (Kerosuo & Engeström, 2003; Tolviainen, 2007). Expansive learning cycles are not developed in a scenario where there is no possibility of discussions, and without expansive cycles, there is no learning (either at individual or collective levels) (Engeström, 1987). In this sense, a potential limitation of CLM is to surmise the existence of equalitarian power relations amid the involved actors.

In the happenstance of an L&D change laboratory, the current study has already served as a preliminary step in which power relations between potential participants have been assessed. In this sense, this study produces knowledge on whether there is scope for a potential CLM in the case of L&D (in terms of dialogue and willingness for open discussion among participants) before the disposition of one.

More broadly, CLM would bring together the findings and discussion laid out in this book and would be the natural next step to a study oriented by activity theory such as this one for the following reasons:

- In legacy interagency interactions, there is a proclivity toward a latent understanding of collaboration (Hean et al., 2009; Hean et al., 2017). Conversely, the CLM focuses on how information is shared across disciplinary boundaries (Kerosuo & Engeström, 2003; Tolviainen, 2007). Thus, the issue of fragmented communication tools (IT systems especially) would serve as a contradiction kicking off a learning cycle to transform the current cycle. Speculatively, the systematisation of interpersonal relationships between front-line workers (as happens casuistically in the current setup) could be proposed as a means to circumvent fragmented communication tools and enable collaboration. In other words, professionals seem to have already developed an efficient way to communicate and collaborate (i.e., through the establishment of one-to-one relationships), so why not let front-line workers come up with ideas on how to build a system around that feature?
- CLM acknowledges that innovation takes place at the interface between disciplines and that working across boundaries is crucial (Engeström et al., 2007). It prioritises the perspective of front-line professionals in addition to leaders with regard to problem identification and solving (Kerosuo & Engeström, 2003), which engenders solutions coordinated at the street level that meet existent needs and do not have to be adapted by front-line workers (Fuglsang, 2010). The horizontal dimensions (wallboards) and vertical dimensions (time) of CLM are designed to unpick what the problem actually is from the mouths of the practitioners in their particular workplace environment (Tolviainen, 2007). In other words, CLM enables the development of bottom-up solutions custom made to the specific needs encountered at the street level.

Current collaborative tools such as care pathways and care plans endeavour to standardise practice as opposed to providing customised solutions such as

CLM. This model of intra- and interagency collaboration allows professionals to work in tandem to resolve issues they have identified as problematic rather than imposing top-down standardised solutions to what management perceives to be challenging, something already proven ineffective (Rittel & Webber, 1973). Thus, it seems logical that a CLM intervention would be the following step to address the findings of this study.

4.5 References

Allen, D., Brown, A., Karanasios, S., & Norman, A. (2013). How should technology-mediated organizational change be explained? A comparison of the contributions of critical realism and activity theory. *Mis Quarterly*, 37(3), pp. 835–854. Doi: 10.25300/MISQ/2013/37.3.08.

Bakhurst, D. (2009). Reflections on activity theory. *Educational Review*, 61(2), pp. 197–210. Doi: 10.1080/00131910902846916.

Cialdini, R. (2016). *Pre-suasion: A revolutionary way to influence and persuade.* New York: Simon and Schuster.

Costa, P. T., & McCrae, R. R. (1992). Normal personality assessment in clinical practice: The NEO Personality Inventory. *Psychological Assessment*, 4(1), p. 5. Doi: 10.1037/1040-3590.4.1.5.

Courpasson, D., & Clegg, S. (2012). The polyarchic bureaucracy: Cooperative resistance in the workplace and the construction of a new political structure of organizations. *Research in the Sociology of Organizations*, 34, pp. 55–79.

Ellström, P. (2010). Practice-based innovation: A learning perspective. *Journal of Workplace Learning*, 22(1–2), pp. 27–40. Doi: 10.1108/13665621011012834.

Engeström, Y. (1987). *Learning by expanding: An activity-theoretical approach to developmental research.* Helsinki: Orienta-Konsultit. Doi: 10.1017/CBO978113 9814744.

Engeström, Y. (1999). Activity theory and individual and social transformation. In Y. Engeström, R. Miettinen, & R. Punamäki, *Perspectives on activity theory* (pp. 19–38). Cambridge: Cambridge University Press. Doi: 10.1017/CBO97805118 12774.003.

Engeström, Y. (2001). Learning at work: Toward an activity theoretical reconceptualization. *Journal of Education and Work*, (1), pp. 133–156. Doi: 10.1080/ 13639080123238.

Engeström, Y., & Escalante, V. (1996). Mundane tool or object of affection? The rise and fall of the postal buddy. In B. Nardi, *Context and consciousness: Activity theory and human computer interaction.* Cambridge, MA/London, England: The MIT Press.

Engeström, Y., Kerosuo, H., & Kajamaa, A. (2007). Beyond discontinuity expansive organizational learning remembered. *Management Learning*, 38(3), pp. 319–336. Doi: 10.1177/1350507607079032.

Engeström, Y., & Sannino, A. (2010). Studies of expansive learning: Foundations, findings and future challenges. *Educational Research Review*, 5(1), pp. 1–24. Doi: 10.1016/j.edurev.2009.12.002.

Fredheim, T., Danbolt, L., Haavet, O., Kjonsberg, K., & Lien, L. (2011). Collaboration between general practitioners and mental health care professionals: A qualitative study. *International Journal of Mental Health Systems*, 5(13). Doi: 10.1186/1752-4458-5-13.

Fuglsang, L. (2010). Bricolage and invisible innovation in public service innovation. *Journal of Innovation Economics*, (1), pp. 67–87. Doi: 10.3917/jie.005.0067.

Fuglsang, L., & Sørensen, F. (2011). The balance between bricolage and innovation: Management dilemmas in sustainable public innovation. *Service Industries Journal*, 31(4), pp. 581–595. Doi: 10.1080/02642069.2010.504302.

Gallouj, F., & Weinstein, O. (1997). Innovation in services. *Research Policy*, 26, pp. 537–556. Doi: 10.1016/S0048-7333(97)00030-9.

Hean, S., Ødegård, A., & Willumsen, E. (2017). Improving collaboration between professionals supporting mentally ill offenders. *International Journal of Prisoner Health*, 13(2), pp. 91–104. Doi: 10.1108/IJPH-12-2016-0072.

Hean, S., Warr, J., & Staddon, S. (2009). Challenges at the interface of working between mental health services and the criminal justice system. *Medicine, Science and the Law*, 49, pp. 170–178. Doi: 10.1258/rsmmsl.49.3.170.

Hean, S., Willumsen, E., Ødegård, A., & Bjørkly, S. (2015). Using social innovation as a theoretical framework to guide future thinking on facilitating collaboration between mental health and criminal justice services. *International Journal of Forensic Mental Health*, 14(4), pp. 280–289. Doi: 10.1080/14999013.2015.1115445.

Hicks, S. (2019). *Explaining postmodernism: Skepticism and socialism from Rousseau to Foucault*. Cleveland: Connor Court Publishing Pty Ltd.

Hill, M., & Huppe, P. (2014). *Implementing public policy: An introduction to the study of operational governance*. London: Sage.

Hornby, S., & Atkins, J. (2000). *Collaborative care: Interprofessional, interagency, and interpersonal*. Oxford: Blackwell Science. Doi: 10.1002/9780470693858.

Høyrup, S. (2010). Employee-driven innovation and workplace learning: Basic concepts, approaches and themes. *Transfer*, 16, pp. 143–154. Doi: 10.1177/1024258910364102.

Hupe, P., & Hill, M. (2016). "And the rest is implementation": Comparing approaches to what happens in policy processes beyond Great Expectations. *Public Policy and Administration*, 31(2), p. 103. Doi: 10.1177/0952076715598828.

Jones, P. (2009). Breaking away from Capital? Theorising activity in the shadow of Marx: Outlines. *Critical Practice Studies*, 11(1), pp. 45–58.

Jones, P. E. (2011). Activity, activity theory, and the Marxian legacy. In *Marxism and education* (pp. 193–213). New York: Palgrave Macmillan.

Keen, J. (2010). Integration at any price: The case of the NHS national programme for information technology. In H. Margetts, Perri 6, & C. Hood, *Paradoxes of modernization: Unintended consequences of public policy reform* (pp. 138–154). Oxford: Oxford University Press. Doi: 10.1093/acprof:oso/9780199573547.003.0008.

Kerosuo, H., & Engeström, Y. (2003). Boundary crossing and learning in the creation of new work practice. *Journal of Workplace Learning*, 15(7/8), pp. 345–351. Doi: 10.1108/13665620310504837.

Lippke, L., & Wegener, C. (2014). Everyday innovation: Pushing boundaries while maintaining stability. *Journal of Workplace Learning*, 26(6–7), pp. 376–391. Doi: 10.1108/JWL-10-2013-0086.

Lipsky, M. (2010). *Street-level bureaucracy: Dilemmas of the individual in public services. 30th Anniversary expanded edition.* New York: Russell Sage.

Ministry of Justice UK. (2013). *Transforming rehabilitation: A revolution in the way we manage offenders.* London: The Stationery Office.

NHS England Liaison and Diversion Programme. (2014). *Liaison and Diversion operation model 2013/14.* London: The NHS Constitution. Retrieved from www. england.nhs.uk/wp-content/uploads/2014/04/ld-op-mod-1314.pdf

Pinker, S. (1995). *The language instinct.* London: Penguin. Doi: 10.1037/e41295 2005-009.

Rittel, H., & Webber, M. (1973). Dilemmas in a general theory of planning. *Policy Sciences,* 4, pp. 155–169. Doi: 10.4324/9781351179522-6.

Robinson, G., Burke, L., & Millings, M. (2016). Criminal justice identities in transition: The case of devolved probation services in England and Wales. *British Journal of Criminology* 56(1), pp. 161–178. Doi: 10.1093/bjc/azv036.

Rocha, P. (2020a). Exploring collaboration within and between criminal justice and welfare systems: The perspective of front-line liaison and diversion workers (Doctoral thesis, University of Stavanger, Norway), ISBN 978-82-7644-960-0.

Rocha, P. (2020b). Where is the primary contradiction? Reflections on the intricacies of research predicated on activity theory: Outlines. *Critical Practice Studies,* 21(2), pp. 6–28.

Rocha, P., & Holmen, A. (2020). Performance-based policy in offender rehabilitation: Limitation or innovation for front-line workers in liaison and diversion services? *Probation Journal.* Doi: 10.1177/0264550520926578.

Roth. (2007). The ethico-moral nature of identity: Prolegomena to the development of third-generation cultural-historical activity theory. *International Journal of Educational Research,* 46(1/2), pp. 83–93. Doi: 10.1016/j.ijer.2007.07.008.

Statham, J. (2011). *A review of the international evidence on interagency working, to inform the development of Children's Services Committees in Ireland.* Dublin: Department of Children and Youth Affairs.

Strype, J., Gundhus, H., Egge, M., & Ødegård, A. (2014). Perceptions of interprofessional collaboration. *Profession and Professionalism,* 4(3), p. 806. Doi: 10.7577/ pp.806.

Styhre, A. (2009). Tinkering with material resources. *The Learning Organization,* 16(5), pp. 386–397. Doi: 10.1108/09696470910974171.

Thunman, E. (2013). Coping with moral stress in the Swedish public services. *Nordic Journal of Working Life Studies,* 6(3), pp. 59–77.

Tolviainen, H. (2007). Interorganisational leaning across levels: An object-orientated approach. *Journal of Workplace Learning,* 19(6), pp. 343–358. Doi: 10.1108/13665620710777093.

Virkkunen, J., Vilela, R., Querol, M., & Lopes, M. (2014). O laboratório de mudança como ferramenta para transformação colaborativa de atividades de trabalho: uma entrevista com Jaakko Virkkunen. *Saúde e Sociedade,* 23(1), pp. 336–344. Doi: 10.1590/S0104-12902014000100027.

Warburton, J., Everingham, J., Cuthill, M., & Bartlett, H. (2008). Achieving effective collaborations to help communities age well. *The Australian Journal of Public Administration,* 67(4), pp. 470–482. Doi: 10.1111/j.1467-8500.2008.00603.x.

Warmington, P., Daniels, H., Edwards, H., Brown, S., Leadbetter, J., Martin, D., & Middleton, D. (2004). *Interagency collaboration: A review of the literature*. Bath: Learning in and for the Interagency Working Project.

Woltmann, E., Grogan-Kaylor, A., Perron, B., Georges, H., Kilbourne, A., & Bauer, M. (2012). Comparative effectiveness of collaborative chronic care models for mental health conditions across primary, specialty, and behavioural health care settings: Systematic review and meta-analysis. *American Journal of Psychiatry*, 169(8), pp. 790–804.

5 Final remarks

This book addresses a gap in the literature of understanding collaboration as a means to innovation in the context of the criminal justice system. Drawing on original research on community-based alternatives to offender rehabilitation, it confirms previous research stating that current models of interagency collaboration are of subpar quality (Hean et al., 2009; Hean et al., 2017) but also provides an up-to-date depiction of the challenges faced by front-line workers at the interface between the criminal justice and welfare services striving to address service-users' needs and provide multifaceted solutions. Above all, the book contributes by identifying existing challenges in the current setup and suggesting alternative solutions to the ones that have been currently applied (Kerosuo & Engeström, 2003; Tolviainen, 2007). The result is the depiction of a scenario in which innovation strategies must prioritise bottom-up–initiated forms of interagency collaboration as a means to provide customised solutions that take into account the peculiarities of the environment and actors involved.

Herein, the point being made is that collaboration between all interested parties, including offenders, is necessary to navigate the system efficiently, since compartmentalised work activities and blockages in information sharing lead to knowledge disparities between agencies and reliance on informal and personal interagency relationships. These structural challenges can be noticed at both intra- and interagency levels despite the existence of policies aimed to promote integration and thereby collaboration (e.g., national models of rehabilitation, diversion and liaison in England and the import model in Norway). Variation in implementation of policies, due to limited time, staff and financial resources, leads to a depreciation in the value given to holistic work activity. Consequently, tensions emerge because of a lack of shared meaning between actors when using workplace tools designed to promote collaboration.

The limitations of current interorganisational arrays are generally recognised in the scientific literature. Especially in the context of offender

DOI: 10.4324/9781003186793-5

rehabilitation, collaboration has to be construed through the lenses of power dynamics, since the way power is held and wielded ultimately alters how agencies work together and whether collaboration is genuinely achieved.

The provision of dignifying response to vulnerable service-users in the community is demanded from the police, but no training is provided to that end. This leads to frustration among front-line police officers and the need for support coming from neighbouring services. Police work has become increasingly complex over time to the point where law enforcement and crime control have nearly become secondary on their list of attributions (Keay & Kirby, 2017). The evidence produced herein points to the increasing number of non-crime-related incidents the police have to address, which is backed up by the literature on the topic. In the UK, non-crime-related incidents account for 84% of calls to the police (College of Policing, 2015), and the situation is similar in Australia, for example, where most of the requests for police presence concern welfare issues (Bartkowiak-Théron & Asquith, 2016). Commentators claim that the police shoulder an unfair amount of responsibility for dealing with vulnerability in the community (Hails & Borum, 2003; Teller et al., 2006), thus the focus of this book on collaborative ways to alter such a scenario.

The effects of overwhelming the police can be clearly perceived in occurrences such as the shooting of Michael Brown in Ferguson, Missouri, in 2014 and the George Floyd case in Minneapolis in the spring of 2020. The Floyd event, especially, has led to a worldwide public outcry asking for major reforms in the criminal justice system and framing the police as an enemy to be defeated. In this scenario, however, it seems more productive to think about how the police can better deliver their services in light of the tremendous discretion they benefit from. Once again, interagency collaboration appears as a commensurate alternative to alleviate the police force and improve service provision. However, it is a given that there is a need for training in methods of collaboration and innovation in the criminal justice staff. As training implies timing, resource and logistical issues, further research should focus on the clarification of the relevance of this type of training for front-line professionals working with offenders in crisis and develop means that suit the busy and complex lives of the professionals involved.

Despite the problems in collaboration, it is inconceivable that security and care are on opposite ends of the continuum, and, therefore, organisations must strive to develop innovative ways in which these can coexist. To that end, this book makes the case for co-created rehabilitation strategies that address the needs of offenders – which can only be achieved with the involvement of health and social welfare services as a means to provide holistic support to individuals – and take into account the dilemmas front-line professionals face to deploy such strategies – which means shifting the top-down paradigm of policy implementation for co-created solutions. Furthermore, the book contributes to an understanding of the challenges facing interagency collaborative practice in the criminal justice system, capturing the front-line professional perspective in this context, which was previously poorly understood.

This book advocates for activity theory because it can support the sensemaking that takes place in these settings, but it is not the only way to promote social innovation and organisational transformation. Despite the theoretical framework adopted, the objective has to be the design of commensurate interventions that give voice to all the interested actors involved in the rehabilitation process. In this sense, future studies can benefit from a multi-theoretical approach that encompasses other perspectives, such as institutional theory and negotiation theory, to explore collaboration in other European and international settings.

For those who embark on this journey through the medium of activity theory, there is an overt need to test methods (such as the change laboratory model suggested in this book) in practice. The CLM can help to achieve cross-boundary collaboration and collective creation of social innovations in organisations facing complex, multifaceted wicked problems, because it empowers the interested parties to deal with the unpredictable, non-linear and emerging nature of practical issues. Since the solutions are developed bottom up by the participants in the CLM, social innovation is naturally achieved via problem identification, co-creation of solutions and implementation and evaluation of new models of working. Having said that, the CLM also has its shortcomings, which reinforces the need for its testing in practice. How can the context-specific solutions produced in each individual CLM be scaled up? How sustainable is the CLM after the researcher has left the institution? What is the emotional burden of the method on those involved in the process, especially in the context of offender rehabilitation, where service-users tend to be in a vulnerable state? How to manage the CLM intervention in high-security environments with vulnerable participants? These are questions to be explored by future research, as the current level of understanding of interventions in the criminal justice setting is still in its infancy, and research efforts must continue so that we can better fathom the benefits of collaborative practice in this context.

In the end, the reader might be wondering what interagency collaboration would look like in a scenario where front-line workers and service-users have a more active voice. While this and other studies suggest that bottom-up solutions are the way to bring organisations together (Hean et al., 2017), more work is necessary to establish the benefits engendered by the implementation of such a solution.

5.1 References

Bartkowiak-Théron, I., & Asquith, N. (2016). Conceptual divides and practice synergies in law enforcement and public health: Some lessons from policing vulnerability in Australia. *Policing and Society*. Doi: 10.1080/10439463.2016.1216553.

College of Policing. (2015). *Stop and search: Guidance for trainers*. Version 1.2, August 2015. Ryton-on-Dunsmore: College of Policing.

Hails, J., & Borum, R. (2003). Police training and specialized approaches to respond to people with mental illnesses. *Crime & Delinquency*, 49(1), pp. 52–61. Doi: 10.1177/0011128702239235.

Hean, S., Ødegård, A., & Willumsen, E. (2017). Improving collaboration between professionals supporting mentally ill offenders. *International Journal of Prisoner Health*, 13(2), pp. 91–104. Doi: 10.1108/IJPH-12-2016-0072.

Hean, S., Warr, J., & Staddon, S. (2009). Challenges at the interface of working between mental health services and the criminal justice system. *Medicine, Science and the Law*, 49, pp. 170–178. Doi: 10.1258/rsmmsl.49.3.170.

Keay, S., & Kirby, S. (2017). Defining vulnerability: From the conceptual to the operational. *Policing: A Journal of Policy and Practice*, 12(4), pp. 428–438. Doi: 10.1093/police/pax046.

Kerosuo, H., & Engeström, Y. (2003). Boundary crossing and learning in the creation of new work practice. *Journal of Workplace Learning*, 15(7/8), pp. 345–351. Doi: 10.1108/13665620310504837.

Teller, J. L. S., Munetz, M. R., Gil, K. M., & Ritter, C. (2006). Crisis intervention team training for police officers responding to mental disturbances calls. *Psychiatric Services*, 57(2), pp. 232–237. Doi: 10.1176/appi.ps.57.2.232.

Tolviainen, H. (2007). Interorganisational leaning across levels: An object-orientated approach. *Journal of Workplace Learning*, 19(6), pp. 343–358. Doi: 10.1108/13665620710777093.

Index

Page numbers in *italics* indicate a figure.

For Product Safety Concerns and Information please contact our EU
representative GPSR@taylorandfrancis.com
Taylor & Francis Verlag GmbH, Kaufingerstraße 24, 80331 München, Germany